Echoes of My Mind

Antonia Urduja Roberts

chipmunkapublishing
the mental health publisher

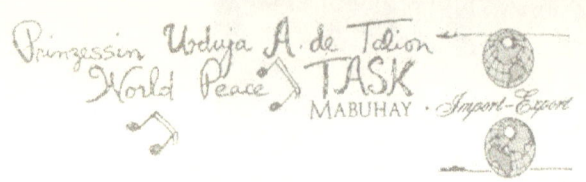

All rights reserved, no part of this publication may be reproduced by any means, electronic, mechanical photocopying, documentary, film or in any other format without prior written permission of the publisher.

Published by
Chipmunkapublishing
United Kingdom

http://www.chipmunkapublishing.com

Copyright © 2016 Antonia Urduja Roberts

ISBN   978-1-78382-236-2

Echoes Of My Mind

Echoes of the past, present and future.... rainbow-coloured world with occasional storms and rainy days, captivating poetry....

Antonia shares her multi-facetted-world filled with challenges to her heart and mind, sometimes heart-rending and mind-boggling, yet immensely inspirational and thoroughly uplifting.

Antonia's private letters to The Queen, Prince Charles, Pope John Paul 11, Pope Benedict XV1, Pope Francis 1 and other important personages in her life and their acknowledgements within the bounds of protocol are revealed herewith..

Antonia is currently promoting The Brotherhood of Man and Mental Health, to eradicate the stigma on Mental Illness.

Explore the uncharted territory of the Mind and Heart of a self-pronounced Princess by raking the graves of her royal ancestors in the Philippines!

Echoes Of My Mind

To my Beautiful and Loving Children and Grandson, I Love You! To my practical Husband, I love you and I need you.

I wish to promote this book toward The Brotherhood of Man and Mental Health. May Love, Forgiveness and Understanding continue to grow in our Heart and Mind, so that Peace may reign all over the World with the passage of Time.

I am deeply grateful to Her Royal Majesty, The Queen, Prince Charles, Pope John Paul 11, Pope Benedict XV1 and Pope Francis 1 who have understood my needs on behalf of the Fulfillment Of the Prophecy Of Our Lady Of Fatima for World Peace.

Mental Health is only an issue toward the attainment of Peace and The Brotherhood of Man is a Pathway toward Peace.

To my dear Readers, I love you and I thank you.

Antonia Urduja Roberts

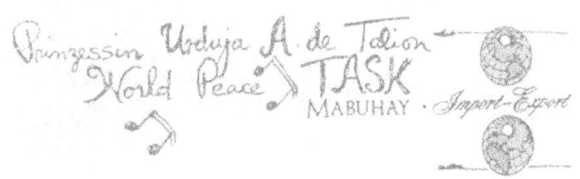

Echoes Of My Mind

Table Of Contents

Chapter I - Rainbows In My Heart and twenty-seven poems written in 2014....

Chapter II - Royal and other Important Letters and Acknowledgements revealed....

Chapter III - Poems written during my pregnancy and labour and other circumstances in the Seventies....

Chapter IV - Essays and Articles written during the OU (Open University), at work as Carer, Bookkeeper and Accountant, Hotel Front Office Cashier and Hotel Night Auditor and in Moments of Relaxation....

Echoes of My Mind

Chapter I: My most recent poems composed in year 2014. Twenty-seven inspirational poems inclusive of Rainbows In My Heart as the opening prayer and a short closing prayer towards the end of the chapter.

1) Rainbows In My Heart - Opening Prayer
2) Summertime
3) Candlelights Endure
4) The Elegance Of Silence
5) Mother, Where Are You?
6) Love In Nature
7) The Almighty Creator
8) Burning Candles In My Heart
9) Bitter Dawn And Glorious Sunset
10) My Vision
11) The Mind Of My Heart
12) The Wings Of My Heart
13) The Cries Of My Heart
14) Anger In Silence
15) Echoes Of Love
16) My Heart In Distress
17) Forgive Me, A Sinner
18) Resolution From My Heart
19) A Chain Of Joy
20) Good Deeds And Prayers
21) My Celestial Home
22) Heartbeats Come Alive and Raindrops
23) Tears Of Sadness, Love And Joy
24) Happy Birthday Today - 2014
25) My Brother Wind
26) Love And Pain
27) Closing Prayer

Echoes Of My Mind

Chapter I

To my cute grandson, Leo Francis born to Sev and Clare Roberts on the 29th July 2015, bringing a mountain-load of Joy in my Heart and Mind. May both of you share extra Joy from me. To my dearly-beloved and beautiful daughter, Elsie Roberts and her ebullient partner, Andy....may the Joy of Love keep you both happily moving forward.

Antonia Urduja Roberts

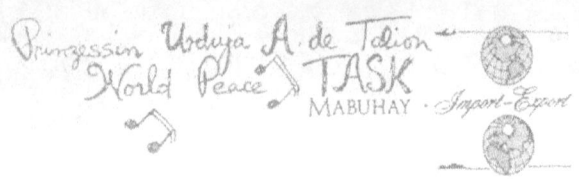

Rainbows In My Heart

Dear Father, Lord God and All!

I bow my head and beseech Thee to help me with my Mind and Heart. Please guide me in my Daily Endeavours especially in my Personal Life. Having been gifted by Thee with two loving children, now grown-up, I want Thee to know that I love them with a pure and unconditional love, with the understanding of their faults and their unawareness and their stages of development as children to adults.

I haven't lost my Way Lord.... at least, not yet. But if Thou didst not come to me now, to Hug me with Thine Love, Care and Protection, I may not find the Way Thou hast intended for me, Lord. I am beginning to feel alone and forgotten even if I am amidst a multitude of people, all-searching for Thine Love, Care and Protection.

Thine silent Love, Care and Protection I do believe in. They are colours within the Rainbows.... the Rainbows that Heal and Purify with the Love in Thine Heart, a Heart that magnifies Truth.... Truth in the Godhead and Truth in Nature and Truth in Human Imperfections.... There are millions of them, but they can be perfected in Thine Divine and Human Love!

Teach me, my God to be Loving, Patient and Gentle-

In all the vicissitudes of my life, be it good or be it bad,
For the good to be better and the bad to be good;
In all my trials and tribulations to develop strength in my character
And a sense of humour in the seriousness of them all,
In the thoughtlessness of my family and friends
For they could be experiencing trials and tribulations
In various events in their lives just as I am undergoing mine;
Nurture my growth from the Sufferings that I meet on
The Way during my Journey of Life unto Eternity.

Let me use the benefits, blessings and good graces
That Thou showereth across my Pathways,
To cheer up those who are ill and suffering,
And to open their eyes on Thine Goodness and Love-

On the Beauty and Wonder of the
Universe, the World and Humanity!

Summertime

Sunshine in the morning,
Sunshine in the evening-
Moonshine at night
With fireflies flickering light.

Trees and plants blossom,
Nourished by the earth's bosom,
Leaves and flowers dance and sing,
While I fly on an angel's wing.

The innate sophistications of the stars,
Strengthen soldiers fighting wars-
And I am mesmerized by their magic
Although I believe that wars are tragic.

World Peace abound through Love of Nature,
Let Earth's beauties Nature nurture-
Behold the summertime joys,
Share them like children's toys.

Candlelights Endure

With candlelights I pray,
Oh Lord, lead me the way-
This extraordinary world promises excitement
For my mind and heart that need enhancement-
So that my intellect will grow in wisdom
And my heart's passions be expressed in your kingdom-

Oh Lord, I pray....
With candlelights I pray,
Oh Lord, don't leave me along the Way,
The wind is blowing
And my heart keeps singing
Waiting for your indestructible Love
To skyrocket me to the stars above-

Oh Lord, I pray...
With candlelights I pray,
At last, I know the way!
The Sun, the Moon and the Stars above,
Invite me with hearts full of Love,
To zoom to the heavens and rejoice
With Natures phenomena of my choice.

Oh Lord, I pray....

With candlelights I pray,
I thank and adore You on my way,
The Stars in the heavens fill me with delight
As the Sun and Moon glow with starlight,
The Sun at morn and the Moon at night,
Brightening my pathways all alight-

Oh Lord, I pray....
Amen

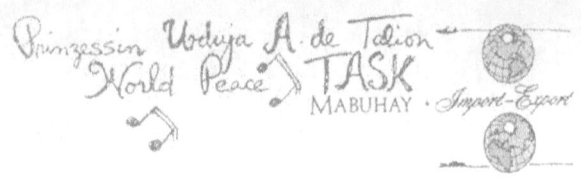

The Elegance Of Silence

Hush- The golden silence emanates from my heart
And I hear the meandering thoughts of the Father.
The love in my heart dances and sings joyfully
Unto the bosom of God's
Being, captivating the
Desires of His Mind and Heart.
My heartbeats shout as the golden silence deepens-
As the atmosphere all around rejoices
And the voices of my heartbeats frighten
The ethereal embodiment of Gods creations.
My mind stretches far beyond my horizons
As my heart's passions ecstatically delight in
The sophistication of the younger generation,
And the promised excitement of this glorious World.
And the silence becomes louder and louder
And lo.... and behold-
The noises of this objective world
Pierce the minds of youth meditating on the
Objective values of the societies wherein they live and exist.
In living, they absorb and ingest the Divinity of God
And the passionate plea of youth for world peace and understanding.
While in existing they beget confusion and incomplete
Growth of their potentials and talents....
A contradiction- for contradiction can be solved
Only by contradiction-
And on the Cross where the Godhead
Jesus was crucified in the golden silence of Calvary,
For on the Cross-, one bar is at variance with another!

Mother, Where Are You?

I push myself forward as I search for you
In my Mind and Heart-
And, I realize that you are a brilliant visionary
But impractical and yet, ahead of your time.
My Heart points at the rainbow,
'There you will find me with all my Love!'
And my Mind says....
'Be not afraid, I will guide you, but be
Careful, you may not find what you are searching for....'
I turn around.... I sing and I dance,
I hope that the gods of my ancestors
Will be lured by my singing and dancing....
And will lead me to you and your Love over the rainbow.
And I regress.... I am a child once again
Crying for your Love and your embrace-
But I see no sign of you
So I cry louder and louder hoping for
Even your shadow to appear.

The rainbow sings and dances with me,
And I keep hoping.... hoping against hope
That you will come, will kiss and will embrace me
Because I love and need you!
There's an emptiness in my heart that is your love-
Your love that is evasive
Because you are busy with your community projects
That sustained your everyday lifestyle,
And I grow once again as an adult in full maturity
Having children of my own
And a husband who pampers me with his love.
Then the rainbow appears once again
And the spirits of your love and your embrace
Jump out and whisper into my ears-
'Forgive me, my Heart is full of love for you,
My darling girl,
But my Mind is in God's hand.'

Love In Nature

Starshine, Moonshine shining at night,
Sunshine holding you to the daylight-
You guide me as I travel the world
In search for my spiritual gold!

You come at night to me, Oh Starshine
Followed by the silver sheen of the Moonshine!
Then, I am so deeply wallowing in my grief-
Because of misunderstandings in my belief.

I follow the rainbow, my sister in spirit
Promising me Wealth of great merit-
My mind meticulously ponders,
While my heart, of your love, often wonders.

Why am I happy, why am I sad?
People often say that I'm bad-
But the language of my heart, is so deeply hidden
In the recesses of my mind, so it can't be trodden.

I peep in the heavens; angels fly to my side....
Globalized angels from far and Wide.
This globalized World of Faith, Hope and Love,
Will be blessed by the heavenly Father up above.

The Almighty Creator

I often wonder where Mother Moon hides herself during the day....
Where Father Sun sets in during the night,
Where Brother and Sister Stars sleep at daylight-

Where....! Who controls their wonderful moments of rest?

Who controls the tides of the oceans
So they won't create a tsunami-
Who controls the volcanoes from erupting
So they won't envelop the earth with lava and fire-
Who controls the each from quakes and thunderstorms
So they won't hasten the end of the world-

Who....! What.... what do we, mere mortals, have to do?

What feelings, emotions and passions should we cultivate?
What world issues should we meditate on
As we transcend the heights of the heavens....?
What flowering plants and trees should we grow
In our gardens…?

What....! Who....! Where....!

The Almighty Creator governs all these things-
And us, mere mortals, must follow,
Adore and thank Him-
So our human follies will disappear
And Peace and Joy on earth will reappear!

Forever and ever. Amen!

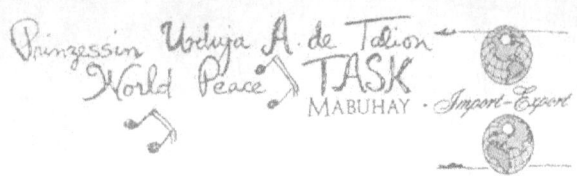

Burning Candles In My Heart

Father and Mother Rain, you
Extinguish the fire of love of the
Candles burning in my heart-
Brother and Sister Rain, come and embrace me,
Bathe me with the sacred raindrops
Falling from the heavens-
Mystify and intrigue my heart and my mind,
Activate them with love, passion and knowledge,
The sanctity of your love will magnify my heart,
The passionate plea of my desires will soften my heart
And the knowledge that you implant in my mind
Will stretch my horizons
Far beyond the limited boundary
Of my human nature's capabilities.

I love....I seek....I desire....
I learn of the tumultuous problems in this
Globalized, modern, civilized societies,
And I seek the pathway to peace,
With the love and desires of my
Indestructible heart of immeasurable silence
But eloquent and sophisticated to be able to
Transcend the invincibility of the immortality of my soul....
My soul within my body-
The God within!

Bitter Dawn And Glorious Sunset

At the break of day is a new beginning
Sweet and bitter is the dawn of life;
In poorer countries with a quest for peace,
Silence reigns in the face of injustice.

My country flourishes in the strength of diversity-
England my beloved!
You nurture diverse communities of people,
Races of various faiths and beliefs.

The dawn of your life continues....
And the sweetness...the bitterness of your day
Are a contradiction-
As the dawn of your life progresses into a
Morning sunshine with the flurry of nature in disarray,
Wind, rain, sun, snow, hail-

Oh glorious day of days!
Why have you done this to me?
Why have you messed me up....
My mind, body, soul and spirit.... why?
Mentally ill, they say, I am-
My own flesh and blood....!
I sing out my heart's desires,
My feelings, emotions and passions....
They threaten me expulsion to Elba
Where the exiled Napoleon met his fate.

Oh Mother and Father Nature,
My solitary voice speaks to the wind!
And the wind is an elemental messenger of
Good and bad tidings!
No one listens to me....
My own flesh and blood laughs at me.
But the Sun, Moon and Stars embrace and caress me,
And my humiliation turns into exultation!

Oh, world of Love, Joy, War and Peace
Of Science, Technology and Globetrotters-
The rich becomes richer, while the poor becomes poorer;

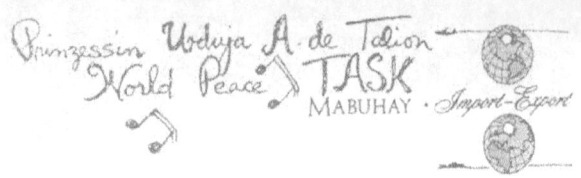

But I am wealthier with my Nature-family,
And, into the glorious sunset I evolve
Ready to stretch the horizons
Of my loving brothers and sisters around the world!

My Vision

I am only a bird flying in the Wind
High up above in the sky-
Growing.... advancing in my mental growth,
Developing my unseen potentials,
Elevating myself towards the
Residences of the gods and goddesses of the Universe.
I am only their servant, their adopted daughter,
Poor and unloved by my Mother when I was a child-
I am a woman of extremes, searching for love in this
Extraordinary World,
Stretching my horizons beyond my limitations.
I am also a Mother, a Grandmother, a Mystic and a Saint-
Indestructible, invincible, immortal....
I am a Spirit with a hundred lives and more!

I become a bird again, flying in the Wind
High up above in the sky.
I mirror the elegance of
God's creations and creatures.
I am humbled, honoured, exalted and exulted
To the very core of my bones-
I am embodied in the visible form of Love.
The delightful sophistication of God's people
Captivate my Heart and my desires,
My feelings, emotions and passions-
I become obsessed....

My health deteriorates
But I push myself forward to the mountaintops,
With a Vision for World Peace
Within the complexity of this globalized World
And I win.... I am alive!

I fly down to Earth
And I become a woman once again,
Brilliant and excited like no one else,
With a dazzling shy smile, I share myself
And I multiply within my Heart and Soul
And the World becomes one with me!

God is Love.... God is Joy.... God is Good....
And I kneel before Him,
Adoring, praying and thanking Him
For the Love He shares with me to share
With this beautiful and fascinating World!

So help me God....! ------ 6th June 2014, 9-10 AM, Friday

The Mind Of My Heart

You are fascination....
You are a shooting star
Landing in my heart from the heavens
As I lay on the silk-gleaming sand on the
Seashore of my beloved hometown
Of Calolbon... the love and joy of my life...!
Gratitude takes control of me and on
This moonlight night with my
Lover lying side by side with me-
I stare at Mother Moon...
And tears of Joy cascade down my cheeks
As ecstasy takes control of my passions,
My feelings, my emotions and my desires!

And the shooting Star uplifts my
Heart to the clouds... the skies and to the heavens!
I commune with the
Angels, the saints and the spirits of my ancestors,
Of my families and friends who are gone before me.
We play in my grandpa's mansion
And I am a little girl once again....
Laughing... singing.... shouting.... running and racing in circles!
Jesus calls me, the Father smiles at me
And the Mind of my Heart becomes
A hiding-place for the Holy Spirit
And Joy conceals herself in my Heart
Strengthening and toughening her,
Imparting courage and wisdom to the Mind of My Heart-
And my Heart is gratified, contented and happy!

My lover complains-
'Where is your Heart, my beloved?'
The shooting star hears him
And she reinstates my Heart back to me.... to my body,
And I continue dreaming
And travelling astrally back and forth to heaven and earth
As my lover kisses me and
Consumes the spiritual vitality of my Heart within my being.
And I take him to mingle with the
Stars, the Moon and the Angels

And we are strengthened...
And happiness fills his Heart, Soul and Spirit.
I continue moving, running and climbing to the mountaintops
For my vision of world Peace
On this highly-technological and civilized-globalized-modern
World that the loving God has entrusted to
Within the hands of Humanity
To develop, cultivate, beautify and to love....

So help us, God!

The Wings Of My Heart

My Heart has a Mind,
My Heart has Wings,
My Heart's Mind thinks for my brain's mind
And overpowers my objective pursuits.
My Heart is sophisticated
And is Oh.... so complicated....
For my Heart's Wings levitate her
Up to the stars when they are
Shining brightly on moonlight nights.
I become subjective in my decisions
And I lean on my Nature-family-
As the gods of thunder and lightning
Frighten the inhabitants of this world,
And interrupts the peaceful existence of humankind.
My Heart is independent of me-
Her wings can spiral me up heavenwards
Or dip me down below to the bottomless
Pit of the ocean and commune with the
Gods of the underworld. To
Excite, befriend, and warn them of the
Tumultuous uproar in the various places on earth,
And for them to beseech the
Firmament to pray for world peace,
For the oneness of divine nature and human nature,
And for the peaceful destiny of humanity!

The Cries Of My Heart

The distant Sunbeams penetrate my heart
And my cries redound to the heavens-
I meet angels and saints at the gate
Hugging and kissing me in joyous expectations!

It's just like earth....!
The past, the present and the future,
The past is gone but the spirit is alive,
The future is way, way ahead-
I am unable to visualize it....
And the present?
I am the present, the here and now
With a frightening shy smile of uncertainty.

My world collapses and I am delighted and fascinated
With the jigsaw puzzle of my life
Sparkling like the morning sunbeams,
That move nearer to embrace
And kiss me like the airy breeze of the summer.

I have to start all over again
And I can't give up now-
I have gone so far from the start of my life
My destiny beckons me with a poignant smile
Moving in deeply within the aortic swimming pool of my heart
Where my feelings, emotions, passions and desires
Take refuge from the harsh objective realities of this
beautiful world !
I kneel in front of the Lord and sing -
But tears contradictorily cascade down my cheeks
And I wonder why I am crying-
Why my joyfulness turns into sadness
Why my destiny is so far ahead of my time,
Why the younger generation captivates my heart
and my mind-
And why.... a hundred and one Whys!
I can't enter heaven just yet-
I have to come back to earth,
To this beautiful and fascinating world
To execute my duties and my tasks!

Anger In Silence

Its ominous, I mean, the silence-
It's so silent in the graveyard,
Corpses silently whispering to one another,
Their voices floating in the air-
Grief still fresh and unabashed,
As silent tears cascade down
Silent faces…benign and malevolent faces!

But a loud crack of thunder booms
And a flash of lightning radiantly
Illuminates the whole graveyard,
And the silent dead are awakened-
In anger they moan,
Their peace.... their sleep.... their precious sleep...
They can't sleep anymore!

Brother Death lingers in the graveyard-
He chastises the awakening-dead,
Mournful that they're disobeying
Nature's law of life and death.
Lucifer, the Bearer of Light, appears,
Sweet as nature's delight-
She smiles and all is forgiven,
Her beauty enthralls the awakening dead-
Their anger, their moans and their mournfulness abate
And silence in the graveyard reigns, once again.
Sleep conquers the living-dead.
There is peace.... their souls and their spirits
Rise up to the stars in the heavens
Along with the reconciled Lucifer
Whose friendship with the Father, the Son and the Holy Spirit
Mitigate the noise, the anguish in war-torn places on earth.

Brother Death conquers the living,
Hundreds and thousands are
Dead in war-torn lands-
Others die of starvation, hunger and diseases,
Some take their own lives!
Oh Brother Death, why are you so cruel?

Echoes of Love

With candlelights I pray,
Oh Lord God, show me the Way,
The day is over, on comes the night
I dream of God's Love, till the morning light.

I feel so tired and worn out,
Yet I feel the need to shout;
I want Your Love-energy
To strengthen my body.

I reflect on my past life
And my duties as a wife,
Oh adorable Godhead,
Be with me, alive or dead.

Come to my heart, explore it,
You'll know when it's full of wit,
I reach for your loving heart,
And from You, I'll never part.

Bestow in my mind, Love-joy,
So with crowds I won't be coy.
I feel your heart in my mind,
And to You I will always bind.

My Heart In Distress

My soul is quiet and still
But my body is quite ill;
I long for You in my heart
I search for You from the start.

I'm aware of Your presence,
But in my heart Your absence
Is a cord of loneliness,
So I search for happiness.

Can I find You in my dreams
As you float in silent streams?
Quiet, still You beckon to me
Clear enough for me to see.

Silently I lift my heart,
Hope from You I'll never part,
I long to kiss You with love
And climb to heaven above.

My Jesus strengthen me
Give me Joy for all to see,
Oh Father and Holy Spirit,
Your Wisdom I may merit.

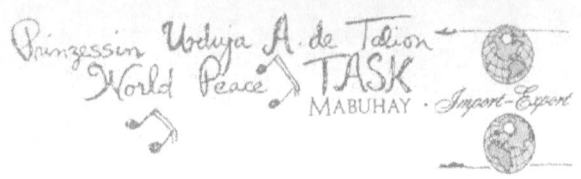

Forgive Me, A Sinner

I feel so disorganized
Day by day in every way-
I think I am about to fall,
But You, my Lord rescues me,
Your majestic beauty guides my pathways
And leads me into the depth of Your Being
Protecting and guarding me.
Your presence creates music in my heart,
And my mind searches for Your wisdom
To connect my body, soul and spirit-
And the faculty of my consciousness and thought
Generates a wholesome persona
To produce peace both in
My heart and in my mind.

How can I purify my being from sins
When all I can think of is physical comfort?
And Your Pain on the cross gets tougher and heavier
As I lose sight of Your sanctity and holiness-
But my Lord, forgive me
Lead me straight into Your embrace
With Your saints and angels make a leeway
With the freedom of Your love.

Resolution From My Heart

Thank You for Your Love, dear Jesus,
Not only in my times of need
For You to strengthen my Heart, Mind and Body
To cope with the atrocities of Life
And to share the best in me to achieve
Peace and Understanding
Amongst people who work for Your Love-
To propagate Faith, Hope and Love in
Your name....
To minimize violence and injustices
In war-torn countries
To seek refuge in the warmth of Your Heart
And be consoled with the
Wisdom in Your Mind....

A Chain Of Joy

Here is my little Heart, dear Jesus
Filled with Love and Joy-
I uplift her with my burning candlelights
In worship and in adoration of Your Kingship.

You have enriched my life, dear Jesus
You have listened to my worries,
Heard my Joys and my Sorrows....
Fill my Heart with the Light of the
Burning candles at my Altar
And fill it with Peace,
Serenity and Joy!

I've searched for You, high and low,
I've climbed mountains, hills, valleys and volcanoes
And peeped into the awesome heavens,
Only to find you resting in my Heart
With the cherubims and seraphims at Your side
Waiting for me to embrace and caress You
With the burning fire of the Love in my Heart!

I then create this chain of Faith, Hope, Love and Joy-
To guide my Pathways to You,
The Father and the Holy Spirit,
To be reconciled to the human nature of the
Angel Lucifer, the Bearer of Light,
So there will be Oneness of the
Divine and Human natures
And a reconciliation of all people within
This Wonderful World!

Good Deeds And Prayers

Such an abundance of natural beauty
Around us- in the heavens and on the earth !
Free to admire, love and to treasure
In our hearts and in our minds.

I kneel before my altar, Oh God
With my candlelights burning.
You descend within my heart and mind
To rest and to reflect
On my Love and on my human weaknesses,
So that I may be strengthened
Body, Soul and Spirit.

I cherish the thought of you
Resting in my Heart,
My most gracious God!
Then I sing hymns of praise, adoration and gratitude.
And I think of war, pestilence and hunger
Around the World besieged by greed,
Selfish power and abomination!

My heart clings to Your Love, Oh God....
And my mind decorates it with
Gold, diamonds, rubies and pearls
Earned by my body's strenuous works and exertions
As I move onwards to share You with
My neighbours and friends and the whole world,
To create Peace and Joy
Through our prayers, kind thoughts and deeds!

My Celestial Home

The ghost of my ancestral home
Lurks behind my Mind all the time-
I am alive in there- a happy child-
Filled with Love and Care
From family, friends and neighbours...
Now, my ancestral home, is gone
Battered by typhoons, storms, strong winds and earthquakes.
That happy child that I am can only
Relive the memories of the
Audacity of my youth
And my most complex complicated Persona,
Destined for a much harder Task for Peace-
Calamities, dangers and hope
Intermingle with each others
Seal my Youth as my Fortitude increases....
As my understanding about life deepens
Within my Heart
And the shallowness of earthly wealth and honour,
Reasons out in my Mind....
As Joy in the Heart of the Lord
Blossoms within my Mind and Heart
And my celestial home turns out to be a
Palace of Faith, Hope, Joy and Love!

Heartbeats Come Alive

You are in a coma,
Heartbeats nearly gone-
The raindrops from the heavens
Come pouring down the hospital roof
And the voices of the angels and their songs
Permeate your heartbeats,
And lo....
You are alive once again!
Your prayers redound to the heavens,
To the Lord, angels and saints!
Their voices and songs echo in your heart
Resuscitating your heartbeats,
Your thoughts and your health....

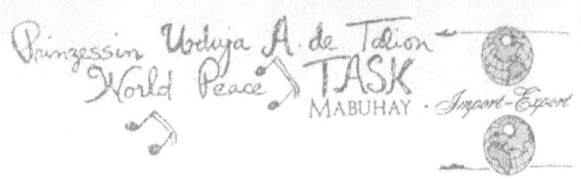

Raindrops

Raindrops are hope and joy to your being
Nurturing the earth, plants and trees-
Raindrops can cheer you up with their music
Pacifying your troubled heart and mind.
Your heartbeats sustain your life.
Day in and day out,
Your heartbeats travel the universe
Imparting love, joy, peace and goodwill.

Tears Of Sadness, Love And Joy

I am alone again tonight,
Like the many lonely nights I have spent,
And in my solitude-
I cry..
Tears telling me to weep deeply,
Tears telling me to smile and laugh,
And tears telling me to shout joyfully
For the coming of my God....

But what are tears made of?
They could be-
Emotions of sadness, loneliness and despair,
Emotions of happiness and love,
Emotions of anger and defeat...
And, what precipitate emotions
But feelings coming from the heart, the mind and
Ultimately, from the nervous system.

I stop crying and my
Heart soars to the skies,
But my mind pulls me down to earth
And my nervous system
Catalyze my feelings and emotions-
And Pride arises from my volcanic heartbeats
Urging my heart and mind to
Symbiotically sing to the Lord-
And my nervous system strengthens my Pride
To continue to execute my
Task for peace of humanity and the world.

And my adrenalin pours
All over my physical body, into my heart and mind-
Through Jesus, my Lord and Redeemer-
Redeemer of love and peace,
Redeeming us from sin.

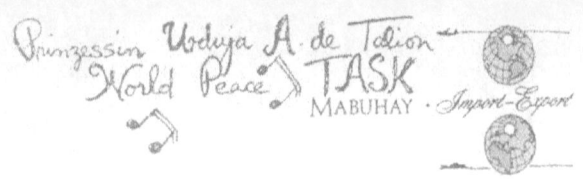

Happy Birthday Today, 2014

Happy Birthday, Elsie!
From the very bottom of my Heart,
I wish you, Elsie, a glorious birthday today.
May your Guardian Angels uplift you from the
Perils of danger in this world-
And may the Virgin Mary lead you unto the
Portals of Joy and Happiness within yourself and others.

Hush, the rain is pouring down heavily
On the roof of my conservatory....
Cold, but not bitter cold-
The heater is besides me
Providing me with warmth
Not just to my body but
Also to my soul and spirit....
Such is western comfort!

May the Joys of this coming winter
And the fun brought about by the snow-white surroundings
Keep you going.
And, may the Love of the Sacred Heart of Jesus
And the comforting arms of His Blessed Mother
Be always with you in Joy and in Pain
Day by day in every way!!!

My Brother Wind

Kiss my heart, Oh Brother Wind,
Kiss my lips, I tell you so-
The sweetness of Your breath
And the love within Your heart
Comfort and sustain me
In my crying times of need!

I love You, Oh Brother Wind
My heart beats with utmost ease
As You swift through to my abode
Cheering me, believing in me and loving me!

My Home, Oh Lover of my loved ones,
Oh yeah Holy Firmament guarding this vaulted arch,
Shielding its mysteries with Your Sword of Courage,
Protecting me, consoling me and hoping in me!

My children, Brother Wind, sweeten them,
Caress them, embrace them, love them-
Enfold them in Your arms and kiss them,
Give them Courage and Strength to battle with Life!

Alas, my Dreams are fewer now,
But the essence within them are solid and strong-
For they have the Wisdom of Love and Contradictions,
And the Supreme One's mystery of Transubstantiation!

Love And Pain

Your Crucifixion is a
Journey of Love and Pain,
Of suffering and sorrow
Redeeming humanity from sin.

A mother gives birth
In Love and in sorrow...
In Joy and in Pain
Intermingling with Hope.

Illumine my pathways, Lord
So I won't go astray.
I need Your Guidance, Love and Warmth
To keep me going till the next day.

You cry blood in Gethsemane,
As You meditate in Love and Pain,
Angel Gabriel brings You the Wine from Heaven-
To strengthen Your Spirit from Pain.

As I transubstantiate Your sorrow from the Garden,
Your Blood pours into my Heart
My Spirit trembles and my Mind breaks,
To strengthen my Being from life's atrocities.

As You carry Your Cross on to Calvary,
You struggle and fall three times
While men shout at You-
Crucify Him, crucify Him, crucify Him!

As You resurrect on the third day,
Your body shines like the Sun,
You ascend into Heaven,
Illuminating Your brilliant Love to Earth.

Closing Prayer

Oh Light of the Heavenly Glory,

Warm my Heart and penetrate

My Mind with Your thoughts

Of Faith and Music to

Intensify the Love both

Within my Heart, My Mind

And My Whole Being

Without reserve.

Amen.

Echoes Of My Mind

Chapter II

The first parts of these Letters and Acknowledgements have very deep and profound spiritual, moral and emotional implications, which may not necessarily be verbally expressed therein. But, the wise and experienced man knows and feels the beauty hidden within the Heart and Mind of the Author/Writer.

The main essence expressed therein is about the EX CATHEDRA Doctrine of infallibility, which only the Holy Father, the Pope have the privilege to declare infallible.

The latter parts are purely Objective in nature that deal with family-matters and day-to-day issues, which may be personal, national and international.

Sad to say, some of them have already passed on to the next life. May they rest in Peace. Amen.

Antonia Udurja Roberts

Echoes Of My Mind

Chapter II

Letters and Acknowledgements from Her Royal Majesty, The Queen, Prince Charles, Pope John Paul II, Pope Benedict XV1, Pope Francis 1, and from other important personages in Antonia's life, within the bounds of protocol, are revealed herewith....

BUCKINGHAM PALACE

26th March, 2015

Dear Miss Roberts,

The Queen has asked me to thank you for your letter of 23rd March, asking Her Majesty for permission to include some letters you wrote to The Queen, in your forthcoming book.

I should explain, however, that this is not a matter on which Her Majesty would either grant or withhold her permission.

It was thoughtful of you to take the time to write as you did and I send my good wishes to you for the success of your book.

Yours sincerely,

Mrs. Sonia Bonici
Senior Correspondence Officer

Miss Antonia Roberts.

BUCKINGHAM PALACE

14th November, 2013

Dear Mrs. Roberts,

I am writing to thank you for your letter to The Queen with which you enclosed a copy of your autobiography.

Your kind thought in sending this publication for Her Majesty to see is greatly appreciated.

Yours sincerely,

Susan Hussey.

Lady-in-Waiting

Mrs A Roberts

16th January 2007

Dear Mr Roberts,

The Queen wishes me to write and thank you so much for the message which you have sent her for Christmas and the New Year.

Her Majesty greatly appreciated your kind thought for her at this time and hopes that you too had a very happy Christmas.

Yours sincerely

Mary Francis.

Lady-in-Waiting

BUCKINGHAM PALACE

6th February 1987

Dear Mrs Roberts,

I am writing to acknowledge your letter to The Queen of 30th January and return, herewith the letter which you enclosed with it.

Yours sincerely,

(MICHAEL SHEA)

Mrs. A. Roberts.

**Your Royal Majesty
Queen Elizabeth II,**

Dear Queen Elizabeth,

I genuflect in front of Thee and I hope you are well and fine.

I am compiling some of my writing materials for my third book, Echoes Of My Mind. As I sort them out, I find copies of my past letters to you, which I would like to include in my book. Herewith four copies enclosed.

I would be very grateful if you could allow me to include them in my book, as I believe, these would help me in my project on Mental Health.

Yours respectfully, humbly, loyally and fraternally in Baby Jesus and Mother Mary,

Mrs. Antonia U. Roberts of the UK

Das humourliche kleine Spatzlein,

Urda von Doutoohland

Thine in the One Supreme Bearer, in Oneness with Almighty God the Father Om Creator, God the Son our Redeemer Jesus Christ, God the Holy Spirit our Sanctificator and the Human Mischief the Reconciled Angel Lucifer all united in the Quadriune God/Goddess, for the Oneness of Divine Nature and Human Nature, for the coming of Gods Kingdom into this World, for the peaceful destiny of Humanity and for the solution to the Mystery of Life Everlasting, forever and ever. Amen.

Prinzessin Urduja A. de Talion

12 December 201 3

**Your Royal Majesty,
Queen Elizabeth 11**

Dear Queen Elizabeth, (in Jesus and Mother Mary's Name)

I have written three times already to His Holiness, Pope Francis 1, including sending him my autobiography with my first correspondence, and I begot only silence from him. I interpreted his silent-acknowledgement as if to say to me- this Transubstatiationary-vision was through you, therefore, the responsibility to promote This Quadriune God/Goddess Doctrine universally is yours to execute. And with the passage of time, I will use my own discretion through the Holy Spirit, on behalf of this Doctrine as Head of the Catholic Church...

Pope John Paul II sent me around six acknowledgements inclusive of two papal blessings. I thought it was ten, that's what I wrote to Pope Francis I. Pope Benedict XV 1 sent me two acknowledgements with enclosed coloured Holy Family pictures. I have written first to the Vatican in 1970 to Pope Paul VI, wherefrom I also begot no acknowledgement. But I am aware that something is "cooking and brewing" in the Vatican on behalf of this EX CATHEDRA DOCTRINE.

Your Royal Majesty, I am nervous and afraid to move-on and promote this Ex Cathedra Doctrine. But both my Heart and my Head advise me that I must move forward.... for God and the World. Please bestow on me an "In Absentia Blessing", with me kneeling with both knees in front of Thee as Head of the Church of England/Anglican Church. I had been Living On A Prayer in my Journey of Faith and Love and I am considerably Grateful for the Divine and Human Guidance I have received from various sources.

Your Majesty, as Head of the Church of England/Anglican Church, wouldst THOU consider propagating this Ex Cathedra Doctrine of the One Supreme Bearer within the worships of the Church openly and universally within the confines of the Church of England/Anglican Church, which would, hopefully, help in the mutual-symbiotic- understanding relationship between the World

and its peoples and the planet Earth, the Objectives and the Subjectives and cultivate the Beauties around us, more fully.

Yours humbly, respectfully, faithfully and fraternally in Jesus and Mother Mary,

Mrs. Antonia Urduja Talion Roberts of the UK

**Her Royal Majesty,
Queen Elizabeth II,
Buckingham Palace, London SWIA IAA**

Your Royal Majesty,
Queen Elizabeth II,
My Dear Queen Elizabeth II-
In Jesus and Mother Mary's names
For the Fulfillment of the Prophecy of our Lady of Fatima for World Peace-

Enclosed herewith are copies of eleven of my recent poems written May and June 2014. They do not follow the contemporary rules and regulations on poetry-writing, but they contain passions, feelings and emotions from my Heart and Mind. I pray, you'd like some of them.

Thank you for visiting Pope Francis in the Vatican.

Thine in the One Supreme Bearer, in Whom Everything is contained and who sustains everything, the Mightiest and the Most Supreme of Them and of Us All Who has both Divine Nature and Human Nature, Whose Divine Nature and Divine Love has borne for all Eternity, the Almighty God the Father, our Creator, God the Son, our Redeemer Jesus Christ, God the Holy Spirit our Sanctificator, Whose Human Nature and Whose Human Love has borne the Human Mischief, the Reconciled Lucifer, the Angel and Bearer of Light, in union with the Church Triumphant, the Church Militant and the Church Sufferings, for the Oneness of Divine Nature and Human Nature, for the coming of God's Kingdom into this World, for the Peaceful Destiny of Humanity and for the solution to the Mystery of Life Everlasting. Amen.

Prinzessin Urduja A. De Talion

Yours good-humouredly, das kleine Spatzlein, the tiny, little Sparrow,

Urda von Deutschland

Yours respectfully, humbly, loyally and fraternally, in Jesus and Mother Mary's names.

12 December 2013

**Your Royal Majesty
Queen Elizabeth 11**

The Fulfillment Of The Prophecy Of Our Lady Of Fatima For World Peace Under
The Spiritual, Tangible And Visible Guidance Of His Holiness Pope Francis 1, Head Of The Catholic Church, And Of Her Royal Majesty Queen Elizabeth II, Head Of The Church Of England/Anglican Church.

My Issues Are:
1) Mental Health - the gradual creation and unfoldment of the wholesomely- holistic-improved World Mentality through Spiritual Globalization.

2) Spiritualism- to be recognized and approved as a Spiritual-Supernatural and Mystical-Science, at par with Psychiatry and Medical Sciences as important in the attainment of Issue I; respecting the first 3 Principles of Spiritualism as a Religion such as The Fatherhood of God, The Brotherhood of Man and Personal Responsibility.

3) The EX CATHEDRA/Infallibility of the Doctrine of the Quadriune God/Goddess instead of just The Triune God...
Of The ONE SUPREME BEARER- in Whom Everything is contained and Who sustains everything, the Mightiest and the Most Supreme of Them and of Us All, Who has both Divine Nature and Human Nature, Whose Divine Nature and Whose Divine Love has borne through all Eternity Almighty God the Father our Creator, God the Son our Redeemer Jesus Christ, God the Holy Spilt our Sanctificator, and Whose Human Nature and Whose Human Love has borne through all Eternity the Human Mischief, the Reconciled Angel Lucifer All united in Oneness with One Another; in Union with the Church Triumphant, the Church Militant and the Church Sufferings, for the Oneness of Divine Nature and Human Nature, for the coming of Gods Kingdom into this World, for the Peaceful Destiny of Humanity and for the solution to the Mystery of Life Everlasting, forever and ever, Amen.

Thine in the One Supreme Bearer, in Oneness with Almighty God the Father, God the Son, God the Holy Spirit and the Human Mischief the Reconciled Angel Bearer of Light Angel Lucifer, for the Oneness of Divine Nature and Human Nature, for the coming of Gods Kingdom into this World, for the Peaceful Destiny of Humanity and for the solution to the Mystery of Life Everlasting, Amen.

Prinzessin Urduja A. De Talion

Yours humourfully, Das Kleine Spatzlein,

Urda von Deutschland

Yours respectfully, loyally, fraternally, faithfully and humbly,
In Jesus and Mother Mary,

Mrs. Antonia Urduja Talion Roberts of the UK

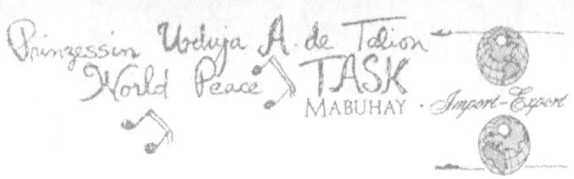

**Her Royal Majesty
Queen Elizabeth 11,
Buckingham Palace,
London w1**

Your Royal Majesty!

Thank You for Your kind letter to me. Yes, I had a very happy Christmas 2006 and New Year 2007. Thank you again.

I thought it would be appropriate for me to send you copies of my two recent correspondences with Mr. Tony and Mrs. Cherie Blair.

I also enclose our recent issue of The Echo where I have a full-paged advert relevant to my issues on Mental Health and a few photographs from one of my little wards down at Upalong Home, Camberley, Surrey- a pre-Christmas dinner-dance-party at "Lost in Atlantis" in Farnborough, Hampshire.

Please allow me to curtsey in front of You and to share with Thee the Warmth of my Heart and Mind in union with Mother Mary and Baby Jesus, for the Fulfillment of the Prophecy of Our Lady of Fatima for World Peace to succeed gradually now and evermore.

Thank you again. I remain

Your Humble and Loyal Subject,

Mrs. Antonia Urduja Talion Roberts of the UK

Das Humourvolle Spatzlein,

Urda von Deutschland

Thine in the One Supreme Bearer, in Oneness with the Quadriune God/Goddess, in union with the Church Triumphant, the Church Militant and the Church Sufferings,

Princess Urduja A. de Talion

1st January 2004

**Her Royal Majesty
Queen Elizabeth II,
Buckingham Palace,
London**

Your Royal Majesty Queen Elizabeth!
Sehr Verehrte Koenigen Elizabeth!
Dear Queen Elizabeth!

Re: The Fulfillment of the Prophecy of Our Lady of Fatima for World Peace

My heartfelt prayerful greetings for this New Year 2004 and Gods Blessings.
Thank You most kindly for Your Christmas message broadcasted on the television.

I enclosed herewith copies of my two recent letters to Prince Charles without the prints of my book of Poems, one of which he had acknowledged . . . and a CV of mine.

I am writing to you to ask for your Blessings in my new and continuous endeavour in life, despite the fact that I will be 60 years old in September 2004. My last letter to You was around December 1992 wherein I enclosed a Christmas card greetings for Mr. John Major with which he thanked me for it, and on behalf of my Ex Cathedra Doctrine of the One Supreme Bearer- Father, Son and the Holy Spirit and the Human Mischief the reconciled Angel Lucifer all united in Oneness with One another, in union with the church Triumphant, the Church Militant and the Church Sufferings . . .for the Oneness of Divine nature and Human nature, for the coming of Gods Kingdom into this World, for the peaceful destiny of Humanity and for the solution to the mystery of life everlasting, Amen.

In February 2004, I would be starting a course with The Open University that would, hopefully lead to a BA/BSc degree in Health and Social Care within three to four years course of continuous studies, with the hope, that it would help me with my personal

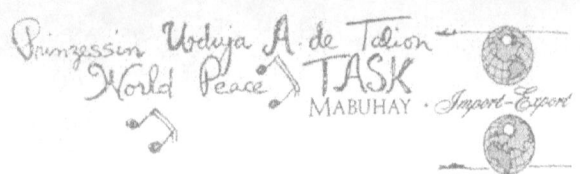

research on Mental Health, Attitudes and Mentalities and other relevant matters to Health and Social Care, in context with the EX Cathedra Doctrine of the One Supreme Bearer . . .that was transubstantiated within me in Cloud Forms way back around November/December 1972, while I was on duty as a Front Office Cashier in the then Skyline Hotel which is now Sheraton/Skyline Hotel by Heathrow Airport.

As Head of the Church of England, I implore Thee to bestow upon me, Thine Blessings in Mind and Heart, an absent blessing with me kneeling with both knees in front of Thee, with my left hand holding a lighted candle and with my right hand over where my heart is. And, hopefully, by the Grace of the Divine Providence of the Godhead, to be directed among the pathways to integrate and harmonise this EX CATHEDRA DOCTRINE of the ONE SUPREME BEARER . . .within various channels, this having been already unofficially acknowledged and blessed by His Holiness Pope John Paul II over twenty years ago, so that it can be realised as the Universal Creed with subsequent Universal Mentality to be nurtured, to be grown and to be cultivated around and within it.

Thine in the One Supreme Bearer . . .Father, Son, the Holy Spirit and the Reconciled Angel Lucifer, in union with the Church Triumphant, the Church Militant and the Church Sufferings.

Yours Humourfully and Kindly, Das kleine Spatzlein,

Urda von Deutschland

Yours faithfully, loyally, respectfully and humbly,

Mrs. Antonia Urduja Talion Roberts

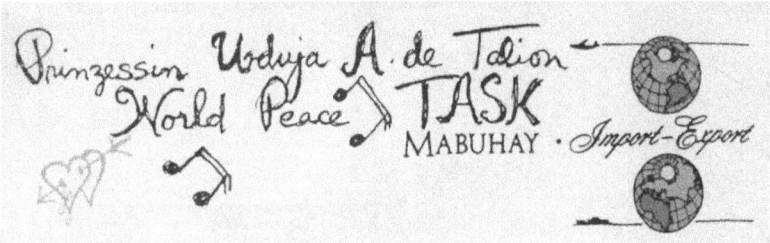

3 December 1995

Her Royal Majesty
Queen Elizabeth 11,
Buckingham Palace,
London

Your Royal Majesty
Queen Elizabeth 11,

Re. Task For The Fulfillment Of The Prophecy Of Our Lady Of Fatima For

W O R L D   P E A C E !

Please allow me to kneel in front of Thee and to bow my head in Thine presence to pay my homage and allegiance as I spiritually regard Thee as the Western representation of the Blessed Mother Mary.

I enclose herewith copies of my letters to my cousin, Governor Severo Alcantara of Catanduanes, my father's friend Senator Francisco Tatad both from the Philippines, the General Secretary of the Catholic Institute For International Relations, Cardinal Hume and to Prince Charles.

I hope and pray in Jesus and the Mother Mary's names that the solutions for PEACE in our troubled world will surface out from our minds to become tangible and real realities.

Please extend to me IN ABSENTIA, Thine Blessings as the Head of the Anglican Church, as I kneel in front of Thee with my praying hands holding my Holy Rosary and one of my Crucifixes.

I am most grateful.......

THINE in the One Supreme Bearer/ Bathala

Princess Urduja H. de Talion
Yours goodhumouredly, Das kleine Spatz, Das Spatzlein !
Urda von Deutschland
Yours loyally, humbly and most sincerely,
Mrs. Antonia H. Roberts of the United Kingdom

CLARENCE HOUSE
LONDON SW1A 1BA

From: Miss Claudia Spens M.V.O.
        The Office of TRH The Prince of Wales and The Duchess of Cornwall

Private and Confidential

15th September, 2014

Dear Miss Roberts,

The Prince of Wales and The Duchess of Cornwall have asked me to thank you for your kind letter of 9th August enclosing a copy of your book, *Lightning Pierced My Heart*.

It was extremely kind of you to send Their Royal Highnesses a copy of the book and they greatly appreciated your thoughtfulness.

The Prince of Wales and The Duchess of Cornwall have asked me to pass on their warmest thanks and very best wishes.

Yours sincerely,

Claudia Spens

Miss Antonia Roberts

CLARENCE HOUSE
LONDON SW1A 1BA

From: Miss Claudia Spens M.V.O.
       The Office of TRH The Prince of Wales and The Duchess of Cornwall

Private and Confidential

29th October, 2014

Dear Miss Roberts,

The Prince of Wales and The Duchess of Cornwall have asked me to thank you for your kind letter and gift.

Their Royal Highnesses are most grateful to you for taking the trouble to send them a copy of your book, Schizo-Whispers. It really was most thoughtful of you and The Prince of Wales and The Duchess of Cornwall have asked me to send you their warmest thanks.

Yours sincerely,

Claudia Spens

9th August 2014

**Your Royal Highnesses
Prince Charles and Duchess Camilla!**

For The Fulfillment Of The Prophecy Of Our Lady Of Fatima For World Peace

I used to write to you years ago, when my mind was unstable, insecure and I was having an identity crisis, which was part of my pathway towards Holistic Growth and development of my Mind and Heart, my mental, emotional and spiritual growth. But the circumstances during those times were relevant to this Task for World Peace- both Subjective and Objective. I also do correspond to Her Royal Majesty, The Queen.

I would be grateful if you would allow me this time to continue writing to you now and then as relevant to this Task for World Peace, the Objective Aspect being- Mental Health and Forgiveness, Globalized Mentalities and the Subjective side is the EX CATHEDRA DOCTRINE of the ONE SUPREME BEARER, which is already in the Hands of Her Royal Majesty, The Queen and Pope Francis. Its Infallibility can be only declared EX CATHEDRA by the Bishop of Romo, the Pope.
Now, I must concentrate on the Objective aspect of this Task. Herewith enclosed is my second book- Lightning Pierced My Heart, contents relevant to Mental Health. I have also sent copies of my first book, Schizo-Whispers, My Autobiography to The Queen and Prince William and Princess Kate, which they have, acknowledge the usual way.

I wish you both Happiness and Joy in your life and may God bless you always.

Thine in the ONE SUPREME BEARER, in Whom Everything is contained and Who sustains Everything, the Mightiest and the most Supreme of Them and of Us all, Who has both Divine Nature and Human Nature, Whose Divine Nature and Divine Love has borne Almighty God the Father, our Creator, God the Son Our Redeemer Jesus Christ and God the Holy Spirit our Sanctificator; and whose Human Nature and Human Love has borne the Human Mischief the Reconciled Angel Bearer of I\Light, Angel Lucifer, all united with

one another...In union with the Church Triumphant, the Church Militant and the Church Sufferings...
Prinzessin Urduja A. De Talion
Das Kleine humomlische Spatzlein,
Urda von Deutschland
Yours respectfully, humbly, loyally and fraternally in Jesus and Mother Mary,
Mrs. Antonia Urduja Roberts of the U.k.

18 October 2014
London SW1A 1AA

Dear Prince Charles and Duchess Camilla!

For the Fulfillment of the Prophecy of Our Lady of Fatima for World Peace

Hope you are both well and fine-.

I enclose herewith my autobiography, Schizo-Whispers, my first book. Lightning Pierced My Heart, which you both kindly acknowledged in a letter is my second book. Hopefully next year, I'll be able to have my third book- Echoes Of My Mind,
published. I also enclose herewith a copy of my letter to Pope Francis, which went unacknowledged. I sent a copy of this to Her Royal Majesty, The Queen, as well as my autobiography, Schizo-Whispers that she lovingly acknowledged not in so many words, that was during the Super Typhoon in the Philippines, last November 2013. I was very moved and grateful, emotionally and spiritually by her kind gesture.

I started writing to Pope Paul V1 in 1971, which begot no reply. Pope John Paul II, as from 1984 must have sent me around six replies to my letters to him and enclosures. Pope Benedict XVI sent me two acknowledgements together with two holy pictures of Baby Jesus and Mother Mary. But I received no acknowledgement at all from Pope Francis. The good Lord must have valid reasons for this.

My books will ultimately lead to my promotion of some issues on Mental Health.
Jason Pegler, the founder/owner of Chipmunkapublishing since 1981, which helps individuals who have mental health problems to publish their own books and give guidance, as Jason had had undergone mental and emotional turmoil like myself.

Please give me through your prayers, kind thoughts and deeds! Some emotional and spiritual support for the objective issues that will befall me in the future, despite my age, 70 years old. Thank you ever so much for your spiritual support in the past- I must have about four letters/acknowledgements from your good self which gave me some strength to carry on, somehow or rather.

Thine in the One Supreme Bearer, in oneness with Almighty God the Father, our
Creator, God the Son our Redeemer Jesus Christ, God the Holy Spirit our Sanctificator and the human mischief the Reconciled Angel Lucifer... in union with the Church Triumphant, the Church Militant and the Church Sufferings, for the Oneness of Divine Nature and Human Nature, for the coming of Gods Kingdom into this world, for the peaceful destiny of humanity and for the solution to the mystery of life everlasting. Amen. Prinzessin Urduja A. de Talion

Yours humourfully, das Kleine, das Spatzlein.

Urda von Deutschland
Yours respectfully, faithfully, humbly and fraternally in Baby Jesus and Mother
Many...

Mrs. Antonia U. Roberts of the United Kingdom

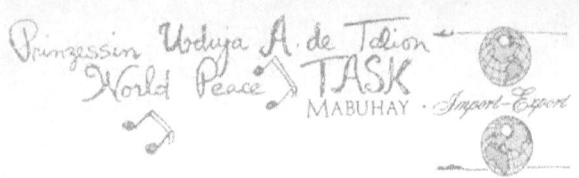

**Your Royal Highnesses
Prince Charles and Duchess Camilla,**

I curtsey in front of you and I hope you are well and fine.

I am sorting out written materials for my third book entitled, Echoes Of My Mind. I am finding copies of my letters sent to you in the past. Herewith I enclose nine pages.

I would be grateful if you would allow me to include them in my book, which hopefully would be a contributory factor for my project on Mental Health, as I am exposing my nervous breakdowns in the past, to help eradicate the stigma on Mental Illness.

Yours respectfully, loyally, humbly and fraternally in Baby Jesus and Mother Mary,

Mrs. Antonia U. Roberts of the UK

Das Humourlische kleine Spatzlein,

Urda von Deutschland

Thine in the One Supreme Bearer, in Ononoos with the Almighty God the Father our Creator, God the Son our Redeemer Jesus Christ, God the Holy Spirit our
Sanctificator, and the Hunan Mischief the Reconciled Angel Lucifer, all united in the Quadriune God/Goddess............

Prinzessin Urduja A. de Talion

I already have a novel on the Ex Cathedra, the Quadriune God/Goddess but the last chapters are somewhat.... not completely right. The title: Lucifer's Fantasy Dream or perhaps Rainbows In My Heart. Please send out some kind thoughts and say a little prayer for me once in a while... Most grateful...

His Royal Highness Prince Charles,
Clarence House,
London

Your Royal Highness Prince Charles,
Dear Prince Charles,

Best wishes for the Easter season and the time thereafter. Hope you and yours are well and fine.

I have written to you several times in the past years on behalf of my World Peace Task relevant to the Fulfillment Of The Prophecy Of Our Lady Fatima. I have received four casual replies from you through your personal secretaries to which I was grateful for. I have rechanneled my spiritual/subjective energies for this Task into spiritual/objective energies to deal with the human needs of the present world. My line of thinking is to concentrate on specificity-of which I have a lot to offer and to share for the benefit of humanity; Mental Health as relevant to my EX CATHEDRA Doctrine of the One Supreme Bearer- the Quadriune God/Goddess as an extension of the Triune God, which had been acknowledged and blessed by the late, His Holiness Pope John Paul II and by the present Pope, His Holiness Pope Benedict XV I, the Catholic Church and the Anglican Church, the spiritual Science as specific within Spiritualism, hand in hand with Psychiatry.

I am working hard to finish my autobiography entitled, Schizo-Whispers, by the end of this year or early next year. I am thinking of founding a charity relevant to Mental Health and my Task for World Peace, in which I'll donate 1/4 of the proceeds of my autobiography as well as in all the other subsequent books. I shall be grateful of your support and I hope it will be alright for me to approach you again within the passage of time.

This time, I am indirectly asking for your sponsorship on behalf of my daughter's Charity - Flora, supposing Cancer Research UK. She's a Runner since she was a little girl. This time, she's running in the London Marathon 2007, on the 22 April 2007. She's training to run in the Olympics Marathon in London during the year 2012. I would, indeed, be very grateful and happy for whatever amount you would extend for my daughter's cause. Would the Duchess of Cornwall, Camilla, be interested in donating, too? I am quite unsure on how to approach her. I hope that I am not trespassing protocol . . .

Thine in the One Supreme Bearer Who has both Divine Nature and Human Nature, in Whom Everything is contained and Who sustains Everything, in Oneness with Almighty God the Father Om Creator, God the Son, our Redeemer Jesus Christ, God the Holy Spirit our Sanctificator, and the Human Mischief the Reconciled, Angel Bearer of Light, Angel Lucifer, in union with the Church Triumphant, the Church Militant and the Church Sufferings, for the Oneness of Divine Nature and Human Nature, for the coming of Gods Kingdom into this World, for the Peaceful Destiny of Humanity and for the Solution to the Mystery of Life Everlasting, forever and ever.

Amen.

Princess Urduja A. de Talion

Yours humourfully, das kleine und schrecklische Spatzlein,
Urda von Deutschland

Yours humbly, respectfully and fraternally,
Mrs. Antonia U. Roberts of the UK

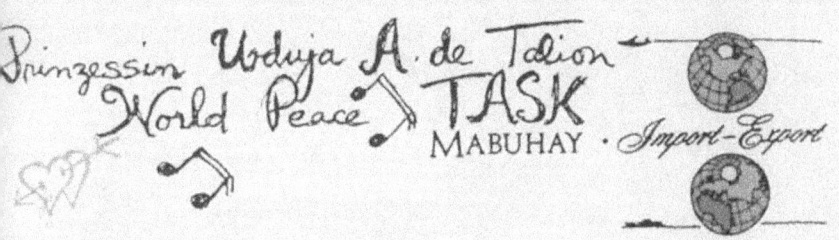

His Royal Highness Prince Charles,
St. James Palace,
London SW1 1BS

Your Royal Highness Prince Charles,
Dear Prince Charles,

RE.   Task For The Fulfillment Of The Prophecy Of Our Lady Of Fatima For

                    W O R L D   P E A C E !

     Please allow me to curtsey, to bow my head before you and to salute
you with the subjective dignity and honour of a Filipina-German-British
Individual Person.

     I enclose herewith copies of my letters to my cousin, Governor
Severo Alcantara, Governor of Catanduanes, to my friend Senator Francis-
co Tatad, to Ian Linden General Secretary of the Catholic Institute For Inter-
national Relations, to Cardinal Basil Hume and to Her Royal Majesty Queen
Elizabeth 11. Also enclosed is a photocopy of the latest letter of my Fili-
pino Spiritual Director, Archbishop Onesimo Gordoncillo.

     Your becoming the future King of your tiny Kingdom as a Role Model for
World Peace is still to become tangible and real. Your love affair with
Mrs. Camilla Parker-Bowles is not frowned-upon by the Blessed Mother who is
the Author of this Idea/Plan of your becoming our future King. You will
read in my letters about my wish/Desire to resurrect Lentheric Morny Ltd.
where I worked in the Operations and Distributions Depart,ments in 1988-
1991 as temporary casual staff- from Smith-Kline and Beechams International.
The Company buildings and factory should be transferred to Catanduanes
on the grounds of our Chalet Farm where we used to have our small holiday
home/chalet. With the Universal Creed of the One Supreme Bearer/Bathala,
the growing Universal Mentality,with Spiritualism as a Spiritual Science,
with my royal pagan ancestry and with my Faith, Hope and Love in the One God,
I shall share with you and others the transubstantiationary nature of the
One Supreme God through Jesus and Mother Mary. Mens Sana et Corpori Sano.
My happy and beautiful childhood memories in Calolbon, Chalet/Timbaan/Lictin
and in Virac, Catanduanes are now resurfacing more clearly and I can now
feel them brewing and alive in my Being.

     I am not knowledgeable about business, although I have some normal ex-
periences-with basics in business bookkeeping and accounting. Therefore, I
should be grateful if your Royal Highness would extend to me a helping hand.
I pray God that your family problems would sort themselves out with the
passage of time.

     With my Kind and loyal regards and best wishes to Your Highness.

Prinzessin Urduja A. de Talion
World Peace ♪ TASK
MABUHAY · Import-Export

   Thine in the name of the One Supreme Bearer/Bathala, in Whom Everything is contained and who sustains everything, the Mightiest and the most Supreme of Them and of Us All, Who has both Divine nature and Divine Love, whose Divine nature and Divine Love borne Almighty God the Father our Creator, God the Son our Redeemer Jesus , God the Holy Spirit our Sanctificatore, whose Human nature and human Love borne the Human Mischief, the Angel Bearer of Light, the reconciled Angel Bearer of Light, Angel Lucifer all united in Oneness with One another, in union with the Church Triumphant, the Church Militant and the Church Sufferings....for the Oneness of Divine nature and human nature, for the coming of God's Kingdom into this World, for the Peaceful Destiny of Humanity and for the solution to the Mystery of Life Everlasting...

               Your spiritual Cousin in the name of Jesus and Mother Mary,

Princess Urduja A. de Talion
Yours good humouredly, Das Vögelein, Das Spätzlein, Urda Von Deutschland

Yours respectfully, loyally, and most sincerely,
Your humble subject —
Miss Antonia U. Roberts
of the United Kingdom

Prinzessin Urduja A. de Tdion
World Peace TASK
MABUHAY · Import-Export

Your Royal Highness Prince Charles,

Sehr Verehrter Prinz Charlie !

Dear Prince Charles,

    I am ever so happy…..please share with my Joy and Happiness that your letter of acknowledgement which I received last Monday, has brought forth into our World Peace Task/Project. You don't know how much that "Courtesy reply" means to me. Of course, I understand protocol… that letter is an inspiration and a motivation factor for me to assert forward my issues on this Task for World Peace and it provides me with a determination to move forward while still looking backwards to my past, for I believe that the past is the foundation and an anchor of the present- subsequently of the future. Here's some of my action plan/issues:
Subjective Aspects- the EX CATHEDRA DOCTRINE of the ONE SUPREME BEARER…..
Objective Aspects-Mentalities, Attitudes and Mental Health Issues, based upon what had happened in my life as well as what is happening in the present.

April/May 1967 = my first Nervous Breakdown in Munich, West Germany while I was living in the Marieluise Schattenmann Heim, Friedrich-Loy Strasse 16, 8 Muenchen 13, West Germany…an international students' hostel for girls. I was then working as a dental receptionist/typist in the American Army Dental Clinic in the Warner Kaserne, Ingostaedterstrasse. I was also attending evening classes in the lower part of the Ludwig's-Maximillian's Universitaet, within walking distance from the Heim, presenting Filipino dances in social clubs, travelling around Europe and my last travel was a 2/3 weeks holiday in Torremolinos/Malaga, Spain, Tanger and Tetuaon, Morocco with my newly-found German girl-friend, Gisela Weidringer. I was also attending Seminars organised by the World University Service and socialising with many international friends of both sexes. And of course, not to forget the most important, I devoured Operas and operettas in theatres within Munich especially during my periods of depression.
When I had my first nervous breakdown in the Heim, I was confined for about two weeks in the Haar Nerven Klinik near or outside Munich. Fr. Luis Jalandoni,a Filipino priest reading for his Doctorate in Theology and a member of my Dance Team- more the coordinator rather than just an ordinary member voluntarily took over the responsibility of being my guardian. My psychiatrist told Fr. Jalandoni that my case was called "Schizo-affective psychosis" And that I should go back to the

Philippines for further treatment and to recuperate. Fr. Luis arranged all my travel documents and paid for my airfare and other travel expenses, organised a farewell party for me with my many friends in the Heim and in the university, a day or so before I enplaned from Munich to Philippines-Manila. He made sure that some of my friends in the Heim came with us to the airport as a farewell party.
Schizo-Whispers is the title of my autobiography.

May 1967 – July 1969 = I was in the Philippines. Confined for a day or so in the San Juan de Dios Hospital by Dewey Boulevard in Manila and was subsequently transferred to the Psychiatric ward of the University of Sto. Tomas Hospital in Manila, where I studied two years Pre-Nursing leading to BSC in the years 1961-62, 1962-63, just before I left the Philippines for the first time to train as a Nurse in a German Hospital in Munich.....Krankenhaus des Dritten Orden, belonging to the Francescan Order of Nuns and Friars- Third Order. The Directors and Directress were friends of my uncle who was then a Catholic Bishop and the then President of the Philippine Mission Society and they were helping him secure monetary donations for the projects he had in his Diocese; schools, hospitals, seminaries, etc. I was confined for a month or maybe two months in the psychiatric ward of the UST Hospital and then I became an out-patient whereby I recuperated in my hometown of Calolbon, now San Andres, Catanduanes and then travelling to Manila again for my out-patient visit with my psychiatrist.

July 1969 – I came back to London to train as a nurse in St. Matthews Hospital, Shepherdess Walk, London EC. I was in London, too, way back in November 1964- until May 1965 (or thereabouts) as a nursing auxiliary in Harefield Hospital, Middlesex while my papers were being processed in the Ludwigs-Maximillian's Universitaet as I wanted to study Medicine, but I had to abandon this idea eventually because I had no money to support me in my studies and I failed the entrance examination. Therefore, I just studied in the language department to enable me to be a German teacher abroad, which of course, I also did not finish because I had my first nervous breakdown in April or May 1967.

October 1969 – I transferred to St. Clement's Hospital in Bow Road, London E, to study Psychiatric Nursing course, after having passed my entrance examination. The Matron in St. Matthews Hospital was displeased with what I'd done but she nevertheless wished me Good Luck.

April or May 1970 = I went to Germany on my own for my allocated holiday or annual leave to visit my German friends. One of them came from that part of Czechoslovakia where Prince Phillip used to live and they were very, very distant relatives of Prince Phillip. Dagmar who I called Daggy really do look like Princess Anne and her brother peter, has a similarity in looks to Your Highness. I met him when he was only 13 years old. Dagmar and I went on Horse-riding lessons in the University Riding school in Schwabing, it was the first time for both of us. She continued it...she used to do so when she was young...and she did very well, including being invited to ride in the Spanish Riding School in Vienna. She was my classmate in the German nursing school. I also visited Gisela and she and her fiancée, Siegfried who was a physics student in the University of Munich invited me to their Hometown in Konfeld nearer the northern part of Germany and I stayed in his parents home with Gisela.

May (/) 1970 = I again had my second nervous breakdown and I had experienced paranormal phenomena which are accepted visions in the Spiritualist religion but not in the medical world. I was confined in the then "The London Hospital" now The Royal London Hospital in Whitechapel Road. I must have been confined in Ansell Ward, the psychiatric unit for about nine months, not that I needed to be there, but because I did not have any relatives here in England. Eventually, Dr. Joe King, my psychiatrist, who was also one of the psychiatrists in St. Clement's Hospital and was slightly besotted towards me while I was still a student nurse in St. Clement's…found a job for me as a filing clerk in the Medical Records Department of The London Hospital and I started there even while I was still living in Ansell Ward. I was never violent nor aggressive. I was mostly singing, dancing, crocheting, knitting, sewing reading, cooking doughnuts, changing myself from one smart dress to another smart dress which I brought with me from the Philippines, spraying my whole body especially my hair with plentiful of colognes and perfumes, especially my favourite Blue Grass, reading, decorating myself with one jewellery and another and another….etc. and eventually, I found a bedsitter in Highgate, commutted to Whitechapel by train for my job in the Medical Records Department, changed bedsitter to Archway,then Wimbledon…took a week or two Hotel and Travel Course in Mendoza's in Oxford Street, got a diploma and started to work as receptionist in Sherlock Holmes Hotel near Baker Street….accepted to work as a Front Office Cashier in the then newly-built Canadian Chain of Hotels-the Skyline Hotel now Sheraton Skyline. I loved it there; it was a second home for me. I was the only Filipina there, I was very popular with everybody from the General Manager to the toilet cleaners, well-liked and was very efficient with an individual sense of humour, worked in all departments in Cashiering- was very happy there but I had moments of depression and I used to lock myself in the toilet and cry silently biting my teeth so my cries won't be heard outside.

- And in November/December 1972, I had this transubstantiationary-vision of the One Supreme Bearer- Ex Cathedra while I was on duty in the Front Office. It was on cloud-forms which transubstantiated within my being…I was on top of the world(delusions of grandeur, so they said)I resigned from my job, telephoned Mr. Vickers who was then the General Manager, asking him to help me send my Ex Cathedra Doctrine to The Queen…to Her Royal Majesty, who I baptised as "Her Illuminated Brilliance, Queen Liz ". Mr. Vickers did not know what the protocols involved in it. Eventually, my then English boyfriend notified the Area Health Authorities and I was eventually confined in the West Middlesex Hospital in Hounslow East for about one month.
- I must have had around 30 Electroconvulsivetherapies, all in all (ECTs)
- My resignation in the Skyline Hotel was not accepted, therefore, after my one-month's confinement in the hospital, I was given back my job. I did write to The Queen after that and I started writing to Pope Paul VI since around 1970 but never received a reply. The first reply I've received was from Pope John Paul 11 way back in around 1981…?
- March 22,1974- I was married to my present husband, Mr. Alan Conway Roberts. November 7, 1976- birth of my first child, Elsie Talion Conway Roberts. I suffered Post-natal depression or medical word for it- Puerperal Psychosis. I enclose a short news and photo of my daughter Elsie, hope you won't mind. These and many more are mentioned in my autobiography.One of the poems in the book I've sent you was written by me when I was in labour with Elsie in the Frimley Frimley Park Hospital way back in 1976.
-
-

My fragmentation and trial in December 1992 which included so many important people -- I thought I'd die. But my resources in the Vatican sustained me and gradually and slowly, my serrated persona had been glued and sewn-up together with very attractive and decorative stitches within my humble and modest self.
•

Thine in the One Supreme Bearer …….. Princess Urduja A. de Talion

Das Humourvoll und schrecklische Spatzlein,   Prinzessin Urda von Deutschalnd

Yours loyally, respectfully and humbly,

Mrs. Antonia Urduja Talion Roberts of the United Kingdom

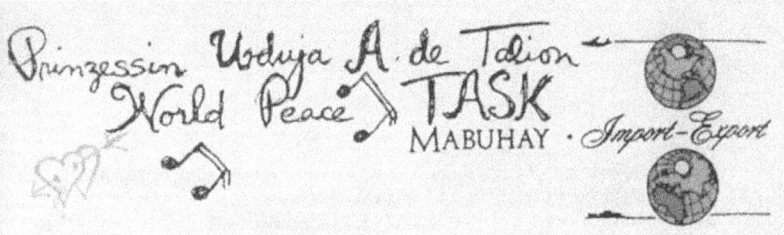

His Royal Highness
Prince Charles
St. James Palace,
London

Re: The Fulfillment Of The Prophecy Of Our Lady Of Fatima For World Peace

Your Royal Highness Prince Charles,
Sehr Verherter Prinz Charlie !
Dear Prince Charles,

It was 1992 when I last corresponded with specific personages on behalf of my Task for World Peace- its essence being my EX CATHEDRA DOCTRINE, which was a transubstantiationary vision sent to me on cloud-forms while I was on duty as a Front Office Cashier in the then Skyline Hotel now Sheraton Skyline Hotel near Heathrow, circa November 1972. It was/is the subjective essence of my Task.

I became fragmented again in December 1992 and it was a long, hard climb to the Objective Realities of the circumstances of my environmental settings. I thought I would die without seeing my Task come into fruition and leaving my two children to bear the burden of its fulfilment. But there are lots of Pathways and Byways that my two children- Elsie Talion Roberts – 26 years old, and Severiano Talion Conway Roberts- 21 years old…..won't know, won't understand and won't comprehend…..ways and means that only my poor and humble self would be able to execute depending upon the circumstances that would prevail now and in the future.

I enclose an up-to-date CV of myself and a printout of some of my poems that I would have had self-published into a book- in fact, I might even have had sent you some of them in the past. Considering the 11-year gap whereby I've transubstantiated, immentalitated, acculturated and inculturated the Objective realities of life surrounding me and in silence, I might even assume that my past tangible correspondences with Your Royal Highness could have been already disposed of and closed; therefore, I should need to open again this Task with Thee, for World Peace…..I won't be able to do it alone ! I shall send a copy of this letter to His Holiness Pope John Paul 11 and a get-well card-message from me. My Objective Reality is full of Contradictions and according to a part of my Elocution piece in my high school years in the Philippines- "Contradiction can be solved only by contradiction,for on the Cross, one bar is at variance with another….."
1994 – started a part-time job as a Care Assistant at Upalong Residential Home, 16 Castle Road, Camberley, Surrey. I left this Home two or three times but I came

back twice and was asked to come back again. Am presently working two nights- 12 hours each night, a week here as a Night Care Assistant.

1995 – started to work part-time nights in Kingsclear Residential and Nursing Home in Park Road, Camberley, Surrey.....worked on days occasionally but I am now on permanent nights working full time- four nights each week, 12 hours each night, overworked and underpaid as people usually comment. I therefore had been working six nights a week with only one night off during the week for over a year now.

When NVQ in Health and Social Care for Carers was made compulsory as a guideline for Care Assistants, I had to train for it and I have only good words to say about it. I've now qualified for my NVQ Level 3, Health and Social Care, City and Guilds. I am currently training for NVQ Level 4 in Health and Social Care as well as for a Managers Award which I hopefully would finish towards the end of November 2003.However, I also have applied to study for a BA/BSc degree in Health and Social Care with the Open University without relinquishing my 6 nights a week jobs. My objective reasoning being- that's the way life's pattern goes in the Objective world. I should need that once I've had my autobiographical novel entitled Schizo-Whispers published. I've temporarily put it aside to give way to my NVQ studies and my 6 nights-job a week. I hope to send it to Harper Collins Publishers in New York, because I used to send my poems and other writing to Harper and Row Publishers in New York in the distant past and they always acknowledged them, even if they were only rejection slips which still gave me the incentive to carry on.

I would, indeed, be extremely grateful in the name of the One Supreme Bearer' Your Royal Highness, if "Thou" could occasionally think of me and send me some kind thoughts and a little prayer for the further development of this Task for World Peace and Understanding. Perhaps, Thou and I could continue to cultivate a Oneness in Faith and Belief in this Doctrine of the Quadriune God/Goddess(please see the prayer towards the end of the poems' printout). We might be able to create with inspiration from the Vatican, new principles of Justice to take over "an eye for an eye, a tooth for a tooth", that Lex Talionis Code of Justice which happen to be my maiden surname. I don't seek objective justice for the injustices that I've had had in my life.....injustices borne out of misunderstanding and unawareness of the objectives, principles, morals and ethics that accompany my actions which may be contradictory to others. I leave them all to the "Lord of All" and His Angels and Spirits.....who guide and show me the ways.....who I lean on to, once in a while, who bless me and who catch me when I am falling and pick me up when I have fallen. My Happiness and Joy dwarf the pains and heartaches and sufferings that I have undergone, but of course, I've understood the unawareness and misunderstandings and misconceptions of the others who inflicted them unto me.

There were two deaths in my family in the Philippines last year, my Father died in February 2002 and my brother, born next to me died in December 2002. Financially, I've got about £50,000=00 debts, loans and credit cards debts.Its very expensive "Growing Up" and the process of the solidification of my fragmented-selves which is also part of my growth to maturity on the western attitudes and mentalities- a conglomeration of Germanic-European, Anglo-Filipino mentalities combined with the diversity of attitudes and mentalities. I've also have had to send monies to my family in the Philippines and donated monies to the church and schools in my hometown, as well as help my children "Growing up", too. I love them very dearly and am very happy and I do love my English husband too, despite all the Contradictions. However, I am not worried about my monetary situation at present.

I've stopped going to Our Lady Queen of Heaven Catholic Church in Frimley, temporarily because there are lots of things I'm trying to discern and understand about religion. My husband, too, who is a Spiritualist- is the West London District Healing Leader, of the "West London District Executive Healing Committee" and his district includes 52 churches. I don't tangibly involve myself in his church duties. He enjoys his tasks here and that keeps him happy, keep him going and keep me happy, too.

I am executing a fairy tale to come into the objective reality of the world; therefore, I must write and act like a fairy tale and this fairy tale is also for the world and humanity to benefit from my fairy tale Task !

Thine in the One Supreme Bearer, in Oneness with the Almighty God the Father, our Creator, God the Son our Redeemer Jesus Christ and God the Holy Spirit our Sanctificator and the reconciled Human mischief the Angel Lucifer...all united in One with one another.....for the Oneness of Divine nature and Human nature, for the coming of Gods Kingdom into this world and for the peaceful destiny of humanity....
Princess Urduja A, de Talion

Das schrecklische und kleine Spatz; Prinzessin Urda von Deutschland

Yours respectfully, loyally and humbly,
Mrs. Antonia Urduja Talion Roberts

KENSINGTON PALACE

From: Miss Claudia Spens M.V.O.
         The Office of TRH The Duke and Duchess of Cambridge and HRH Prince Henry of Wales

Private and Confidential

27th August, 2014

Dear Mrs. Roberts,

The Duke and Duchess of Cambridge have asked me to thank you for your kind letter and gift.

Their Royal Highnesses are most grateful to you for taking the trouble to send them a copy of your book, *Lightning Pierced My Heart*. It really was most thoughtful of you and The Duke and Duchess of Cambridge have asked me to send you their warmest thanks and best wishes.

Yours sincerely,

Claudia Spens

Mrs. Antonia Roberts

KENSINGTON PALACE

From: Miss Claudia Spens M.V.O.
        The Office of TRH The Duke and Duchess of Cambridge and HRH Prince Henry of Wales

Private and Confidential

5th September, 2013

Dear Miss Roberts,

The Duke and Duchess of Cambridge have asked me to thank you for your kind letter and gift.

Their Royal Highnesses are most grateful to you for taking the trouble to send them a copy of your book, Schizo-Whispers My Autobiography. It really was most thoughtful of you and The Duke and Duchess of Cambridge have asked me to send you their best wishes.

Yours sincerely,

Claudia Spens

Miss Antonia Roberts

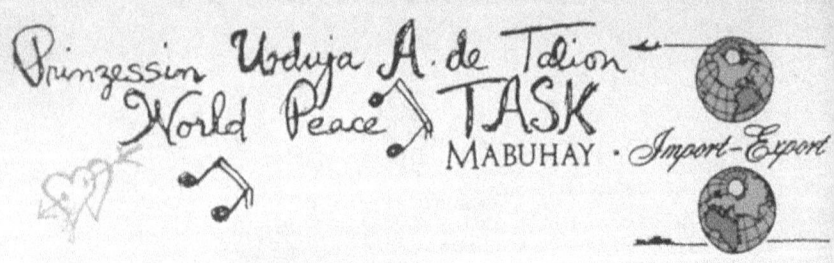

Their Royal Highnesses
Prince William and Princess Kate

For The Fulfillment Of The Prophecy Of Our Lady Of Fatima For World Peace

I am, indeed, very happy for your Family, more especially Prince George.,

I enclose herewith my second book- Lightning Pierced My Heart. My first book- Schizo-Whispers, My Autobiography had already been sent to you and acknowledged in the usual way.

My Task for World Peace as above; both the Subjective and Objective. The Subjective side which is that of the EX CATHEDRA DOCTRINE of the ONE SUPREME BEARER, I have already handed in into the Hands of Her Royal Majesty, The Queen and to the Pope. The Pope being the only one who can proclaim Ex Cathedra to the Universal World and the Infallibility of the Doctrine. Now, I must concentrate on the Objective Aspect of this Task- Forgiveness and Mental Health and Globalized Mentalities. I value and need your Spiritual Support, once in a while for this World Peace Task. I am very grateful.

Thine in the One Supreme Bearer in Whom everything is contained and Who sustains everything, the Mightiest and the most Supreme of them and of us all, Who has both Divine Nature and Human Nature, Whose Divine Nature and Divine Love has borne for all eternity the Almighty God the Father our Creator, God the Son our Redeemer Jesus Christ and God the Holy Spirit our Sanctificator; Whose Human Nature and Human has borne the Human Mischief the Reconciled Angel Bearer of Light, Angel Lucifer in union with the Church Triumphant, the Church Militant and the Church Sufferings....

Prinzessin Urduja A. de Talion

Das kleine, humourlische Spatzlein,

Urda von Deutschland

Yours respectfully, humble, loyally and fraternally in Jesus and Mother Mary

Mrs. Antonia Urduja Roberts of the UK

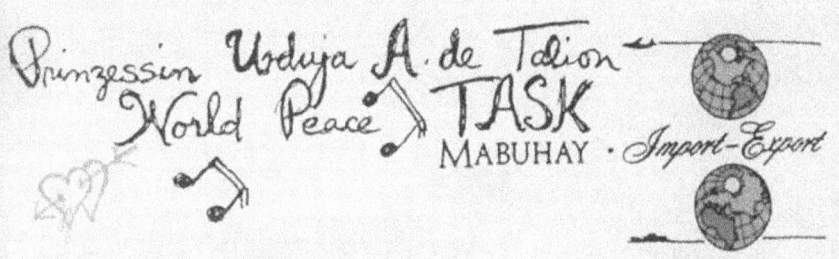

Their Royal Highnesses
Prince William
Princess Kate
Prince George,
Kensington Palace
London

Your Royal Highnesses
Prince William !
Princess Kate !
Prince George !

Re: Fulfillment Of The Prophecy Of Our Lady Of Fatima For World Peace- The
    EX CATHEDRA Doctrine Of The Quadriune God/Goddess

Enclosed herewith is my Prayer on behalf of the EX CATHEDRA Doctrine of the Quadriune God/Goddess which Transubstantiated within me way back in November/December 1972 while I was on evening duty as a Front Office Cashier in the then Skyline Hotel which is now the Sheraton/Skyline Hotel by Heathrow Airport.

I first wrote to His Holiness Pope Paul V1, way back in 1970, but it was only in 1981 when I first received an acknowledgement from His Holiness Pope John Paul 11. In the course of my Journey, I must have received around six to eight replies acknowledgements from His Holiness Pope John Paul 11, two from His Holiness Pope Benedict XV1, two from Her Royal Majesty The Queen, three or four from Prince Charles and one or two from other important personages in other parts of the world, in the course of time. I had my uncle in the Philippines who was a Catholic Bishop as my Spiritual Counsellor and upon his death, I had a Filipino Archbishop-friend who became my Spiritual Counsellor.

I also enclose herewith my autobiography.

Meanwhile, I am writing my second book on the EX CATHEDRA, working two nights a week as a Night Care Assistant in a small residential home for eight residents in Camberley, Surrey, caring for my seventy-six year old English husband who had just had a coronary arterial triple bypass in September last year and for another year or so, I hope to retire from my night care assistant's job and then consolidate so many of my writings about my experiences in care homes since 1993 and write another book about it.

I pray that this EX CATHEDRA Doctrine will eventually Unite the Church of England and the Catholic Church in future and be proclaimed as Infallible by the future Pope in our slow journey to World Peace.

I pray for Their Royal Highnesses for Their continued blessings from the Almighty God.

Thine in the ONE SUPREME BEARER, in Whom Everything is contained and Who sustains everything, the Mightiest and the most Supreme of them and of us all, Who has both Divine Nature and Human Nature, Whose Divine Nature and Divine Love had borne for all Eternity the Almighty God the Father, our Creator, God the Son our Redeemer Jesus Christ, God the Holy Spirit our Sanctificator; Whose Human Nature and Whose Human Love has borne for all Eternity the Human Mischief the Reconciled Angel Lucifer, all united in Oneness with one another, in union with the Church Triumphant, the Church Militant and the Church Sufferings; for the Oneness of Divine Nature and Human Nature, for the coming of God's Kingdom into this World, for the Peaceful Destiny of Humanity and for the solution to the Mystery of Life Everlasting forever and ever. Amen.

Yours humourfully, Das Spatzlein,

Yours humbly, respectfully, loyally and fraternally in Baby Jesus
        and Mother Mary,

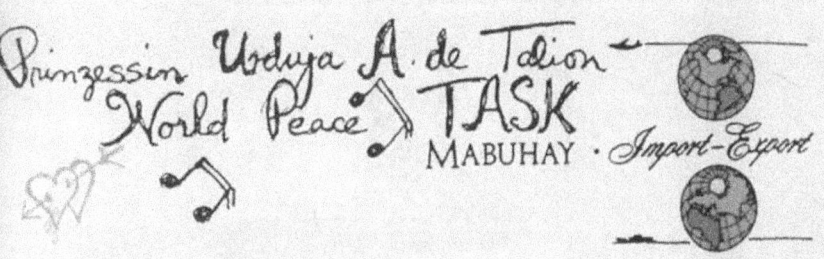

Their Royal Highnesses
Prince William, Princess Kate and Prince George,

For the Fullfillment of the Prophecy of Our Lady of Fatima for World Peace

Thank you for the acknowledgement-letter you sent to me on behalf of the receipt of my autobiography, Schizo-Whisper, some while ago.

Herewith enclosed are eleven of my poems written May and June 2014. They do not follow the contemporary rules and regulations of poetry-writing, but they contain passions, feelings and emotions from my Heart and Mind. I pray you'd like some of them.

I'm always happy to see and read news about the Royal Family, especially of the younger generation, moreso because I also have grown-up children belonging to this generation. And, I always send out some kind thoughts and prayers especially for your family.

    Thine in the One Supreme Bearer, in Oneness with Almighty God the Father, our Creator, God the Son our Redeemer Jesus Christ and God the Holy Spirit, our Sanctificator, and the Human Mischief, the Reconciled Angel Lucifer, Angel Bearer of Light; in union with the Church Triumphant, the Church Militant and the Church Sufferings; for the Oneness of Divine Nature and Human Nature, for the coming of God's Kingdom into this World, for the Peaceful Destiny of Humanity and for the solution to the Mystery of Life Everlasting. Amen.

Prinzessin Urduja A. De Talion

Yours good-humouredly, das kleine Spatzlein, the tiny little Sparrow,

Urda von Deutschland

Yours respectfully, humbly, loyally and fraternally in Jesus and Mother Mary's names,

Mrs. Antonia U. Roberts of the United Kingdom

10 DOWNING STREET
LONDON SW1A 2AA
www.gov.uk/Number10

From The Direct Communications Unit

26 November 2013

Ms Antonia Urduja Roberts

Dear Ms Roberts

The Prime Minister has asked me to thank you very much for sending him your book, 'Schizo Whispers My Autobiography'.

Mr Cameron really appreciates your kind thought and is most grateful for your support and good wishes.

Yours sincerely

Correspondence Officer

10 DOWNING STREET
LONDON SW1A 2AA

From the Direct Communications Unit

2 February 2007

Mrs Antonia Urduja Roberts

Dear Mrs Roberts

I am writing on behalf of the Prime Minister to acknowledge your recent letter and the enclosures.

Yours sincerely

G EDWARDS

10 DOWNING STREET
LONDON SW1A 2AA

From the Direct Communications Office   18 December 2006

Mrs Antonia Urduja Roberts

Dear Mrs Roberts

The Prime Minister has asked me to thank you and your co-signatories for your recent letter and the enclosures.

                               Yours sincerely

                               M DAVIES

Prinzessin Uduja A. de Tdion
World Peace **TASK**
MABUHAY · *Import-Export*

28th January 2007, Sunday

Mr. Tony Blair,
10 Downing Street,
London

Dear Mr. Blair,

Re: The Fulfillment of the Prophecy of Our Lady of Fatima for World Peace

The EX CATHEDRA Issue of the ONE SUPREME BEARER- in Oneness with the Quadriune God/Goddess- the Almighty God the Father, our Creator, God the Son our Redeemer Jesus Christ, God the Holy Spirit our Sanctificator; and the Human Mischief, the Reconciled Angel Lucifer, the Bearer of Light...in Union with the Church Triumphant, the Church Militant and the Church Sufferings...for the Oneness of Divine Nature and Human Nature, for the coming of God's Kingdom into the World, for the Peaceful Destiny of Humanity and for the Solution to the Mystery of Life Everlasting, now and forever, is ekking to come out into the Open. Amen.

The Location where the Transubstantiationary-Vision was given Birth was in the then Skyline Hotel, now Sheraton-Skyline Hotel near Heathrow Airport, while I was on late, evening shift duty as a Front Office Cashier in December 1972. This circumstance could provide various important themes and questions to different minds of different people in the Government and in the Church. The fact that this was given birth not in a Church but in a 5-Star hotel, significantly implied the Objectivity of this Doctrine. The Quadriune God/Goddess has chosen to be Objective in the midst of this Ailing Humanity.

What are the Legal and Moral implications if this Ex Cathedra Doctrine is passed or voted as a Universal Creed through the English/British Parliament? The fact that this Doctrine which imbues Rights and Privileges, Duties and Responsibilities, Legal and Moral Values which we need to nurture and cultivate within us as a Nation and as Individual Human Beings, should be encouraged and sought for, for Unity and Mutual Understanding.

But, the message was Catalyzed through Me-a Filipina. (I was not married yet, I was still a Filipina citizen, then. I was married in March 1974 to my present husband.) will put my country, the Philippines in the map. It was in the Vatican where I relied most for my Spiritual Support- the Rock of St. Peter sustained me.. "I was the Voice of One crying in the Wilderness...." Several 'moonlight-rendezvous with Father and Mother

Nature, Brothers and, Sisters Nature and all their Children also sustained me Via the Rock of St. Peter to search for "…the Light at the End of the Tunnel…" Faith and Prayers sustained me, too. "Faith can move mountains." "Pray without ceasing."

What Action would the Vatican take if this Objective Doctrine is superimposed over and above the Christian Religion and the Triune God? And, be proclaimed as a Universal Creed in Great Britain? An extension of the already prevailing one.

The Tree that would grow by subsequent proclamations and acceptances of this Doctrine would bear multitudinous orchards of wealth, talents and knowledge of the future….both Subjective and Objective, that would Overpower war and violence and greed. Anger and hatred would need to be forgiven and perhaps, even forgotten. Revenge should not be nurtured in our Hearts and Minds. Unselfish Sharing would become a way of life

What moral and legal rights and privileges, duties and responsibilities, legal and moral values are we going to be subjected to, as a Nation and as inhabitants of Great Britain as this Universal Doctrine permeates our Beings?……That's enough for the moment; I am on night duty and my residents need some Caring.

Is there any possibility, Mr. Blair, that You could stay a few more years as Prime Minister to nurture and provide growth to this Ex Cathedra, Objective Baby-Doctrine; I feel that I have an excellent rapport with THEE…., and to guide us to be able to cultivate relevant Issues so that we would be able to cope reasonably well with the Changes and more Changes in this Modern World for our Children and our Children's children, and so on and so forth…

Thine in the One Supreme Bearer, in Oneness with the Quadriune God/Goddess, in Union with the Church Triumphant, the Church Militant and the Church Sufferings…

Princess Urduja A. de Talion

Das Humourvolle und Schrecklische Spatzlein,

Urda von Deutschland

Yours humbly, respectfully and cordially,

Mrs. Antonia Urduja Roberts of the UK.

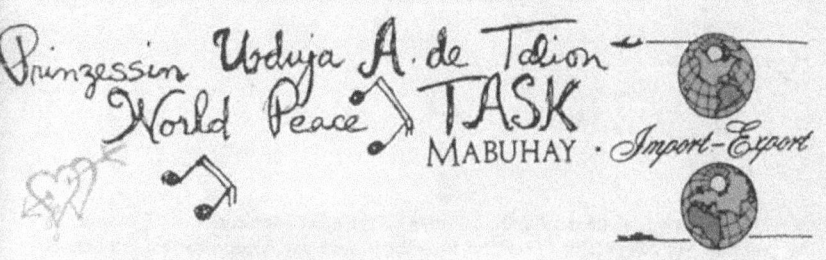

9th December 2006-12-11

Mr. & Mrs. Tony & Cherie Blair,
10 Downing Street,
London

Dear Mr. Blair,

Re: The Fulfillment Of The Prophecy Of Our Lady Of Fatima For World Peace

Thank You ! A Big Thank You !! A Giant Thank You !!!

Thank you for visiting His Holiness Pope Benedict XVI, inviting him to visit England, relevant to my latest renewal letter to Her Royal Majesty Queen Elizabeth 11, requesting for a renewal inner-spiritual strength and support, as Head of the Church of England, so that I could slowly execute the Objective Aspects of The Prophecy for World Peace and Understanding.

A Big Thank You for your Message last night, broadcasted on television, relevant to being British- about the Rights and Privileges, hand in hand with the Duties and Responsibilities on matters of Integration and Multiculturalism. And British Tolerance !

- A Giant Thank You for being Britains Prime Minister. And with this, may I ask you to "say a little prayer and send out some kind thoughts for me", on behalf of my Research on Mental Health, allied to Universal Mentality, using my Life and my Life Experiences as the "Guinea Pig". Part of this is included in my three-quarterfull autobiography.

My Thank Yous also go to Madame Cherie for being a Great Wife to a Great Prime Minister and a Model Mother and Career Woman.

I enclose herewith a copy of my EX CATHEDRA Prayer which was unofficially Acknowledged and Blessed by His Holiness Pope John Paul 11; the main Substance of this Prayer occurred in a Transubstantiationary-vision written on Cloud Forms to me, while I was on evening duty as a Front-Office Cashier in the then Skyline Hotel, now Sheraton-Skyline Hotel near Heathrow airport, way back in late November or early December 1972. I also enclose a few recent photographs of myself and my family. And, a Christmas prayer in a small Christmas card for you and your dear Wife Cherie and family.

Way back on Christmas 1992, I've written to The Queen and enclosed a Christmas card for Mr. John Major. This Christmas Wish was acknowledged with a short casual business-like reply from Mr. John Major. May I ask Thee this favour?

    THINE in the ONE SUPREME BEARER, in Whom Everything is Contained and Who Sustains Everything, the Mightiest and the most Supreme of Them and of Us All; Who has both Divine Nature and Human Nature, Whose Divine Nature and Divine Love borne Almighty God the Father our Creator, God the Son, our Redeemer Jesus Christ, God the Holy Spirit, our Sanctificator, Whose Human Nature and Human Love borne the Human Mischief, the Reconciled Angel Lucifer, all United in ONENESS with One Another. In Union with the Church Triumphant, the Church Militant and the Church Sufferings, for the Oneness of Divine Nature and Human Nature, for the Coming of God's Kingdom into this World and for the Solution to the Mystery of Life Everlasting forever and ever. Amen.

Prinzessin Urduja A. de Talion

Das kleine und humourvolle Spatzlein,

Urda von Deutschland

Yours respectfully with humility in Union with Baby Jesus and Mother Mary,

Mrs. Antonia Urduja Talion Roberts

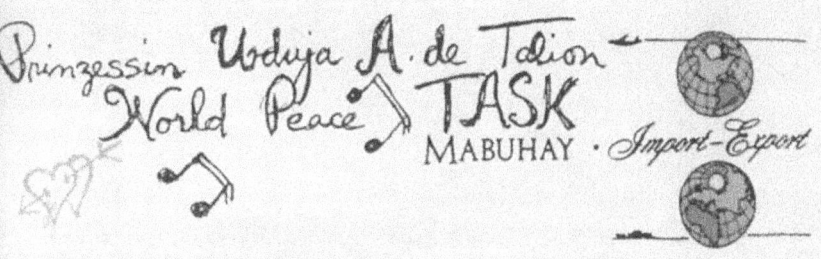

Dear Mr. Blair & Madame Cherie !

May Peace and Joy. be with You both this New Year 2007.

Thank you for your acknowledgement on behalf of my communication with you which included Best Wishes for Christmas 2006 and the New Year 2007. I also received a beautiful and warm letter from Her Majesty, The Queen and a spiritually-uplifting letter from the Pope which informed me of my file number in the Vatican archives and a beautiful photograph of the Holy Family with a message in Latin at the back and a signature of Pope Benedict XVl

These and all the other things in my life, without forgetting my family who I consider as God's gift to me, made/make me, indeed, extremely happy. Thank you again.

Herewith enclosed is a rough-draft of my next full-paged advert in The Echo, a free magazine of the Our Lady Queen of Heaven Catholic Church in Frimley (Spring/Summer issue- out around May 2007).

Please allow me to put forward some of my thoughts, some of which may appear ridiculous to you, now. I am writing for the future...

In Great Britain, wherein the Government overpowers the Church, where legality is above morality, where Tolerance and Fairness are the marks that distinguish us from other Nations,...would The EX CATHEDRA DOCTRINE of The ONE SUPREME BEARER be superimposed as a Creed wherefrom Legality and Morality or vice-versa, Tolerance and Fairness be catalysed as the basis for the 'Gradual Changes' in Government Laws and Legal system relevant to Immentalitation, Inculturation and Integration?

In the Catholic Church, this Ex Cathedra Doctrine of Papal Infallibility, can be validated and be declared only by the Pope. The fact that this happened to me in December 1972... a poor and humble, little Sparrow- is still beyond the comprehension of ordinary mortals. But, my Mother is of royal, ancestral lineage which dated back to the Divine Rights of Kings. And, if this Doctrine permeate the Church of England, which would be gradually incorporated in the Changes within the Government- Universal Creed and Universal Mentality.....well, I don't think I can carry on any longer; it needs too much thinking power and thought-energy.

Although my Father was a a barrister, a politician, writer and poet, singer and dancer, elocutionist and orator, etc, and I have inherited some of his political philosophies,and some of his talents, yet I am only an Ignoramus in English and British politics." I only know what I know" sang Frank Sinatra. A little bit of this, a little bit of that...I only know, a little.

Talking about my Ignorance, I went to see Fr. John,(Parish priest of OLQH church) after the Holy Mass the other day to give him photocopies of Your letter to me,to the Pope's letter to me, as well a copy of this enclosed copy of my Ex Cathedra doctrine for my next advert in The Echo. He greeted me with a mischievous smile and remarked that I am "in competition with St. Paul with my Epistles..."I used to give him copies of my poems, my essays with the Open University, short stories, et al. But I told him that he is included in my Ex Cathedra doctrine as it is a Universal Doctrine and that the One Supreme Bearer is eeking to come out into the open. As well as my unfinished autobiography, I also have another unfinished novel about the One Supreme Bearer and the Quadriune God/Goddess instead of the Triune God. Funnily enough, the Manager of Kingsclear Homes,in Camberley, Surrey where I work as a night carer for two nights , makes fun of my letters to her calling them as 'Epistles, too.' I just laugh...I don't get angry.
" So, laugh loud and long...
While working for success to
Come along...."was a part of my Father's poem.
I hope you'll laugh loud and long at the "untidiness" of my issues in this letter and not get angry. That's my main object- to allow you to laugh and ease-up all your tensions and stress!!! That's my German-self...the Urda in me. If you haven't laughed or giggled or smiled, you haven't fathomed yet my "German-Spatzlein" mentality. That's one lecture in Immentalitation...

This Celebrity-culture all over the world is getting out of hand, one of the many causes of extreme poverty in many parts of the world. Although, the Right to Compete as promulgated by the Treaty of Rome is healthy, yet this Right is abused in so many ways. My kind regards,

    Thine in the One Supreme Bearer, Princess Urduja A. de Talion

      Das Humourvolle Spatzlein, Urda von Deutschland

        Yours respectfully and humbly, Mrs. Antonia U. Roberts of the UK

18th January 2007

SECRETARIAT OF STATE

FIRST SECTION   GENERAL AFFAIRS

VATICAN CITY

29th November, 1989

Dear Mrs. Roberts,

His Holiness Pope John Paul II has asked me to acknowledge your letter, together with the enclosures, which are returned herewith.

Yours sincerely,

Monsignor C. Sepe
Assessor

SECRETARIAT OF STATE

FIRST SECTION - GENERAL AFFAIRS

No. 47.500   From the Vatican, Christmas 2006

His Holiness Pope Benedict XVI gratefully acknowledges the greetings sent to him for Christmas and the New Year. He appreciates the kind sentiments expressed.

Upon all who remembered him during this holy season he cordially invokes an abundance of joy in Christ the Prince of Peace. He cordially imparts his Apostolic Blessing.

Gabriele Caccia
Monsignor Gabriele Caccia
Assessor

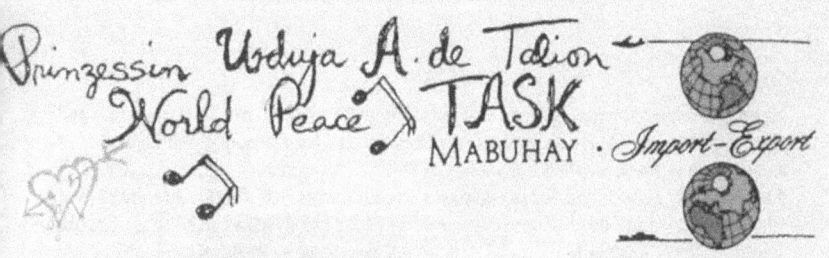

17 August 2004-08-17

Your Holiness Pope John Paul 11 !
Ihren Heiligen Papst Johannes Paulus 11 !
My dear Pope John Paaul 11 !

For the Fulfillment of the Prophecy of Our Lady of Fatima for World Peace !

My husband told me that You went on a pilgrimage to Lourdes as a Pilgrim praying for the improvement of Your Health !

How about me asking you to consult your specialistdoctor if it would be safe for You to have a fortnightly injection of Depixol 20 mg. ? Parkinson's disease is also an illness of the nerves aside from all the other reasons which I do not know about.

In 1976, when my first child was born here in England, I suffered from post-natal depression and other nervous troubles. I'd been prescribed this injection by a Sri Lankan psychiatrist in around 1978. This has been my lifeline. It has preveted me from having strokes on some occasions. It is good for my memory and is one of the medications that I have. I experimented on myself and disobeyed my doctors on the time-prescription for my injection and dosages of the injection and self-decided when and how much to inject within me. I've absoluved them from the responsibility in case something drastic happened to me and assured them that I would be responsible for myself. My reason being-I wanted to know what circumstances had brought about my need to have the injection. My father, being a lawyer and a politician and my uncle, being a Catholic bishop in the Philippines (may they both rest in peace !)...in court cases and in confessionals- the nature of the crime as well as the nature of the sins ; the verdict and the guilt are determined by the circumstances surrounding the crime and the guilt. There was a time when I wanted to withdraw from the injection and for about nine months I did not have the injection. I thought I would die.... And on other times...but that was when I was younger and my children were younger, too. Now that I am older (I'll be 60 years old next month), cured of my post-natal depression, I've self-decided not to withdraw from the injection. And a few nerve-tablets...but the time and dosages are also self-determined by me. Only my high-blood pressure tablets are taken by me once a day as prescribed by my doctor. I cultivate good relationships with my doctors and they have due respect for me. My doctors administer the injection.

Part of how I've survived was through the letters and enclosures I've sent to Thee...in the Vatican and the various casual acknowledgements which You have sent to me gave me strong spiritual graces and my faith in the good Lord(in Baby Jesus and Mother Mary, in nature as well as on other things, (I am very childlike and passionate in these matters), my EX CATHEDRA doctrine and prayers which Thou hast casually acknowledged in the past through letters. My friend, Archbishop Onesimo Gordoncillo of Capiz, Roxas City, Philippines, who I used to escort around Munich, West Germany while he was on holiday, staying in the Krankenhaus where I was then training as a Krankenpflege Schulerin in the years 1963-1965, he was then reading for his Doctorate in Theology in the Colegio Seminario de Filipino on Rome- was my Filipino Spiritual Director when I was ill with nerves. I asked him and he kindly obliged to be so. He occasionally sends me a short note with blessings from the almighty. These were some of my subjective armours in curing myself. The Depixol injection, et al were/are some of my objective tools for getting cured and getting better.

Maybe, in the name of Baby Jesus, Mother Mary and my EX CATHEDRA doctrine and prayers, this Depixol injection may improve or even cure you. We have 2 clients in the Nursing and Residential Homes where I work as a Carer who are over a hundred years old ! I have also asked from Her Royal Majesty, The Queen for her silent blessings for this Task for World Peace. Prince Charles is also one of my Patrons. I have written loads and loads of letters and sent enclosures to them and others, in the past and have received casual acknowledgements and these gave me strength and courage in pursuing this Task for World Peace...alone but not alone...!

My daughter is now 28 years old and my son, 23 years old. Both are University graduates. I work five nights a week in 2 residential and nursing homes. I am presently studying for BSc/BA degree in Health and Social Care through distance learning in the Open University. I have had to open myself to the changes...diversified cultures and mentalities and especially to the ways of the younger generations of today. I've succeeded and I am succeeding. One of my pathways and goals is a research on Mental Health...mentalities, attitudes, emotions, feelings, intuitions and others, that's why I am studying for a degree with the Open University because the culture nowadays is to have some letters after one's name in order to be qualified and be an authority in some ways in some academic matters. I am (was and am) following Mr. John Major's policy when he was still the Prime Minister of "Back to Basics."

Please, can You elevate Archbishop Onesimo Gordoncillo's position in the Catholic Hierarchy to be a Cardinal? I would be happy and grateful . Thanks in advance.

I am enclosing herewith a copy of my EX Cathedra Prayers which Thou hast acknowledged and blessed in the past, in case my file in the Vatican had been neglected. I am also sending a copy of this letter to Her Royal Majesty, Queen Elizabeth 11 and to Prince Charles.

Thine in the ONE SUPREME BEARER, in union with the Church Triunphant, the Church Militant and the Church Sufferings...for the Oneness of Divine Nature and Human Nature, for the coming of God's Kingdom into this World, for the Peaceful destiny of Humanity and for the Solution to the Mystery of Life Everlasting, Amen.

Das kleine Spatzlein von Deutschland, Yours humourfully,

Yours respectfully, affectionately and fraternally

Mrs. Antonia Urduja Talion Roberts of the United Kingdom

SECRETARIAT OF STATE

FIRST SECTION - GENERAL AFFAIRS

N. 77.900   Christmas 2007

His Holiness Pope Benedict XVI is pleased to acknowledge the kind message sent to him for Christmas and the New Year. He very much appreciates the sentiments expressed.

Upon all who have greeted him during this holy season His Holiness invokes an abundance of joy and peace in Christ the Redeemer.

Monsignor Gabriele Caccia
Assessor

Prinzessin Usduja A. de Talion
World Peace TASK
MABUHAY · *Import-Export*

His Holiness Pope Benedict XV1,
Vatican City, by Rome
Italy

FULFILLMENT OF THE PROPHECY OF OUR LADY OF FATIMA

FOR WORLD PEACE...

YOUR HOLINESS POPE BENEDICT XV1 !
DEAR POPE BENEDICT XV1 !

Please allow me to communicate with Your Holiness in **PEACE**. Its been a long time since I've written to Pope John Paul 11. I am seeking for a renewal of my correspondence with the Vatican, as I have done so in the past, as a member of the Church Militant, and, on behalf of the Fulfillment of the Prophecy of Our Lady of Fatima for World Peace. I pray in my own little ways that we will all be guided by **DIVINE PROVIDENCE...**

I enclose herewith an updated version of my curriculum vitae and a copy of my **EX CATHEDRA Prayers** which had been acknowledged unofficially and blessed by His Holiness Pope John Paul 11. The essence within these prayers is the doctrine of the **ONE SUPREME BEARER** which was transubstantiated to me in cloud-forms while I was on duty, one evening- as a front office cashier in the then Skyline Hotel, now Sheraton-Skyline Hotel near Heathrow Airport, London, way back in either November/December 1992. I have started writing to the Pope since 1970, but the first reply to my letters was by Pope John Paull 11, in 1984. I got married to an Englishman on the 22 March 1974, in the civil registry office and on the 22 March 1985, my husband and I were married in the Catholic Church by my uncle in his diocese, the then Bishop of Dumaguete City, Negros Oriental, Philippines.

My uncle, the late Bishop Epifanio B. Surban of the above diocese, was my long-distance confessor. However, when I had my post-natal depression, I've requested an old friend of mine since 1965, who is presently the Archbishop in the Archdiocese of Capiz, Roxas City, Philippines,to be my long-distance Filipino Spiritual Director. In 1965, he was then a priest reading for his Doctorate in Theology in the Colegio Seminario de Filipino in Rome and was invited to stay in das Krankenhaus Dritten Orden, Nymphenburg, West Germany in Munich, where my uncle, the Bishop was a good friend of the Francescan Friars and Nuns of the Francescan Third Order. I was then a 19-year old Filipina nursing student in this hospital. I was asked to escort Fr. Onesimo Gordoncillo (the present archbishop) together with my cousin, Fr. Edmundo Surban who was his colleague in the seminary as student-priests, around Munich as they were on holiday together in Munich.

Please allow me to recommend him to be upgraded as a Cardinal. My reason being- I still am in contact with him through correspondence. Normally, I send him printed matters of Catholic magazines, some of which may not be found in the Philippines, such as Catholic Life, as well as local churches' news around here. I write occasionally to him if there's anything necessary to be written about. His upgrading would also upgrade my mental and spiritual mentality outlook and his continuous prayers and moral and spiritual support for me on behalf of this Task for World Peace would continue to grow. This Ex Cathedra doctrine would be the answer to religious plurality and religious diversity around the world. I shall continue my correspondence with the Vatican when there is a need to do so, sometimes just a need for mental clarification on behalf of these issues.

I would, indeed, be very, very grateful for whatever developments, Your Holiness would act upon, on behalf of this Prophecy and Task for World Peace.

THINE IN THE ONE SUPREME BEARER, in ONENESS with Almighty God the Father, our Creator, God the Son, our Redeemer Jesus Christ, God the Holy Spirit, our Sanctificator, through the Divine Nature and Divine Love...and the Human Mischief, the Reconciled Angel Lucifer, through the Human Nature and Human Love in the ONE SUPREME BEARER---for the Oneness of Divine Nature and Human Nature, for the coming of God's Kingdom into this World, for the Peaceful Destiny of Humanity and for the Solution to the Mystery of Life Everlasting, Amen.

Prinzessin Urduja A. de Talion

Das Humourvolle, kleine Spatzlein,

Urda von Deutschland

Yours loyally, respectfully and affectionately in Jesus and Mother Mary,

Mrs. Antonia U. T. Roberts

4th September 2008

His Holiness
Pope Benedict XV1,
Vatican City,
By Rome,
Italy

Your Holiness Pope Benedict XV1 !
My Dear Pope Benedict XV1 in Baby Jesus
      And Mother Mary !

For The Fulfillment Of The Prophecy Of Our Lady Of Fatima For World Peace

  I pray that you are well and fine.

I enclose herewith my first book- Schizo-Whispers: My Autobiography. I also enclose a photocopy of the letter from my Filipino Spiritual Director since 1986. I had post-natal depression when my first child, a daughter was born in 1976 which got somewhat better with the birth of my second child, a son, in 1981. Circumstances happened that I thought I would die- in fact, I have had the Holy Viaticum administered to me at home by the Catholic priest and nun in the Our Lady Queen of Heaven Catholic Church in Frimley, then.

Please, Your Holiness, I beg you to kindly consecrate and elevate the Archbishop Onesimo Gordoncillo to become a Cardinal. This would be a pathway towards a greater understanding of the Ex Cathedra Doctrine of the One Supreme Bearer. I am objectively focusing my research on Mental Health and Mentalities. At present, I am increasing my quota on travelling. But, I still work at my age, 64 years, as a Night Carer in a Residential Home of 9 residents for three nights a week with occasional overtime.

Thine in the One Supreme Bearer, in Oneness with the Almighty God the Father our Creator, God the Son, our Redeemer Jesus Christ, God the Holy Spirit our Sanctificator and the Human Mischief the Reconciled Angel Bearer of Light, Angel Lucifer- for the Oneness of Divine Nature and Human Nature, for the Coming of God's Kingdom into this World and for the Solution to the Mystery of Life Everlasting, Amen.

Princess Urduja A. de Talion

Dein Humourvolle Spatzlein,

Urda von Deutschland

Yours respectfully and humbly,

Mrs. Antonia Urduja Talion Roberts of the United Kingdom

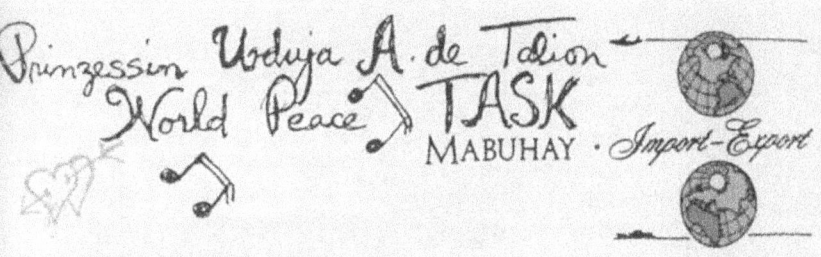

His Holiness
Pope Benedict XV1
Vatican City,
By Rome, Italy

Your Holiness Pope Benedict XV1,

Thank You for Your Apostolic Blessing, Your kind letter and the beautiful picture of the Holy Familia with Your message at the back.

I pray that You had a very Happy and Joyful Christmas 2006 and New Year 2007. I was on night duty on Christmas Eve 2006 and New Year 2007. I watched the celebration of New Year 2007 in London, on television, as well as in various parts of the World. I cried ever so loudly with extreme Joy and Happiness which filled the lounge and the dining room of the Home where I work. But, all my 9 Residents were fast asleep in their respective suites.

And, lastly, my Heart and Mind were/are full of Gratitude to Our Creator Who gave me Life. I feel Honoured and Grateful to have been given the Privilege for the Execution of the Task for the Fulfillment of the Prophecy of Our Lady of Fatima for World Peace, despite all of my Human Imperfections and Human Failures and Mountainloads of Pains and Heartaches. But, I've read long ago in a prayer book, that "Sufferings are the Clouds that come along with the Nearness of God, for God does not come in Clear Shining....."

Herewith are some enclosures relevant to my/our Task for World Peace.

Yours respectfully and humbly,

    Mrs. Antonia Urduja Talion Roberts of the UK

Das Humourvolle und Schrecklische Spatzlein,

    Urda von Deutschland

Thine in the One Supreme Bearer, in Oneness with the Quadriune God/Goddess in union with the Church Triumphant, the Church Militant and the Church Sufferings,

    Princess Urduja A. de Talioni

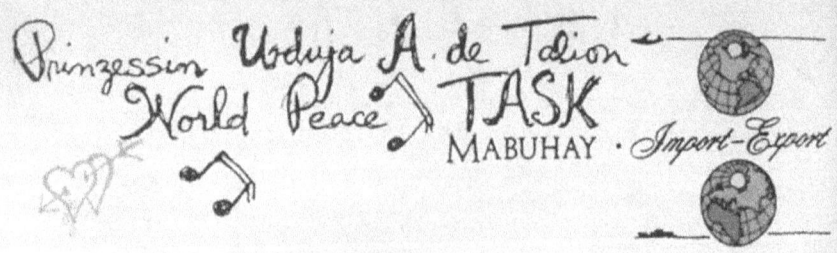

His Holiness Pope Francis 1 !
Vatican City, by Rome,
Italy

His Holiness Pope Francis 1 !
My Dear Pope Francis 1 !

I approach Thee with great Decorum, Humility and Spiritual Love in the name of Jesus Christ !

My first letter to the Vatican was in 1971 to His Holiness Pope Paul V1. The first reply from the Vatican which I received was from His Holiness Pope John Paul 11, in 1981. I have had several letter-replies from him throughout his time as Pope and these replies have had given me the spiritual strength to carry on with the vicissitudes in my life. The Issue which I wish to maintain is the EX CATHEDRA, the Infallibility in the Catholic Church which Thee alone as Pope has the Power to proclaim as Infallible Doctrine in the Universal Church.

I enclose herewith my EX CATHEDRA Prayer of the One Supreme Bearer-

The essence of this Doctrine was revealed to me and transubstantiated within me in Cloud Forms way back in November or December 1972, while I was on Evening duty as a Front Office Cashier in the then Skyline Hotel, now Sheraton Skyline Hotel near Heathrow Airport, London, England. I was then single, living in a bedsitter near the hotel and I was confined in the West Middlesex Hospital in Hounslow East, in the psychiatric Ward for one month...

I got married to an Englishman on 22 March 1974. I have two children, a girl of 36 years and a boy of 32 years. My uncle was a Catholic Bishop in the Philippines. My husband who is 75 years old is a Spiritualist. His father was a Spiritualist Minister and President of the Spiritualist Church in Cowes, Isle of Wight, England. I support the Universality of the Catholic Church. But, as I lived on with my life in a legal country since 1969, I have individually upheld the Interdenominationality of this EX CATHEDRA. But, I did not preach it and I have FAITH in it. I am still waiting for the Pope to declare it officially in his own right and free will, as the Infallible Guardian of the Universal Church.

I pray to God, through Jesus Christ and the Holy Spirit for Thine Infallible Guidance in matters of the Doctrine of the Universal Church. Please say a little prayer for me, too, occasionally to the Holy Spirit for Guidance.

Thine in the ONE SUPREME BEARER, in Oneness with Almighty God the Father, Our Creator, God the Son, Our Redeemer Jesus Christ and God the Holy Spirit, our Sanctificator. And the Human Mischief, the Reconciled Angel Lucifer all united in Oneness with One Another. In Union with the Church Triumphant, the Church Militant and the Church Sufferings, for the Oneness of Divine Nature and Human Nature, for the coming of God's Kingdom into this World, for the Peaceful Destiny of Humanity and for the Solution to the Mystery of Life Everlasting, forever and ever. Amen.

Prinzessin Urduja A. de Talion

Yours Humourfully, Das Spatzlein,

Urda von Deutschland

Yours respectfully, loyally and faithfully,

Mrs. Antonia Urduja Talion Roberts

Prinzessin Urduja A. de Talion
World Peace TASK
MABUHAY · Import-Export

His Holiness Pope Francis 1 !
My Dear Pope Francis 1 !

Is this what it takes for World Peace?

Its high time now that the Highest Hierarchy on Earth should proclaim universally the universality of the EX CATHEDRA- the INFALLIBILITY of the ONE SUPREME BEARER – in Whom Everything is contained and Who sustains Everything, the Mightiest and the most Supreme of Them and of Us all, Who has both Divine Nature and Human Nature, Whose Divine Nature and Whose Divine Love has borne for all Eternity, Almighty God the Father, Our Creator, God the Son Our Redeemer Jesus Christ and God the Holy Spirit Our Sanctificator; Whose Human Nature and Whose Human Love has borne for all Eternity, the Human Mischief the Reconciled Angel Lucifer All united in Oneness with One another, in union with the Church Triumphant, the Church Militant and the Church Sufferings. For the Oneness of Divine Nature and Human Nature. For the coming of God's Kingdom into this World, for the Peaceful Destiny of Humanity and for the Solution to the Mystrery of Life Everlasting. Forever and ever. Amen.
Which was TRANSUBSTANTIATED through within me in November/December 1972, while I was on duty as a Front Office Cashier in the then Skyline Hotel which is now Sheraton Skyline Hotel near Heathrow Airport, London.
Before worse disaster than that of the Philippines happen.

Thine in the ONE SUPREME BEARER,
Prinzessin Urduja A. De Talion

Yours Humourfully, Das Kleine Spatzlein,
Urda von Deutschaland

Yours respectfully, fraternally, humbly and loyally,
Mrs. Antonia Urduja Talion Roberts

Prinzessin Urduja A. de Talion
World Peace ♪ **TASK**
MABUHAY · Import-Export

His Eminence
Cardinal Basil Hume,
Westminster Cathedral
Near Victoria Road,
London

Dear Cardinal Hume,
Your Eminence Cardinal Hume,

Re. Task For The Fulfillment Of The Prophecy Of Our Lady Of Fatima For

W O R L D   P E A C E !

Since this is the first time that I am writing to Your Eminence, I wish to Implore for an IN ABSENTIA Personal/Individual Blessings from You as I kneel before You with my Praying hands holding my Holy Rosary and one of My Crucifixes.

Likewise, I implore again from Your Eminence an IN ABSENTIA Blessings for "PRINCE CHARLES and Myself" with Prince Charles standing by my left side, four steps ahead of me and in whichever positions HE would WISH to assume with HIS Hands ! Whereas, my Humble Self will retain the same kneeling position as in my personal/individual blessings.

Please have the Flags of the Vatican, United Kingdom, Germany, United States of America and of my beloved Philippines adorn the Chapel/church where the Blessings will take place to be performed.

I enclose herewith copies of my letters to my cousin, Governor Severo Alcantara of Catanduanes, etc. Also enclosed is my EX CATHEDRA Prayers blessed and acknowledged by the Pope.

Please allow me to greet you most kindly by kneeling in front of you and kissing your RING as symbol of your Hierarchy. I am most grateful.

THINE in the One Supreme Bearer/Bathala,

Princess Urduja A. de Talion,
You goodhumouredly, The little
Birdie, Das kleine Spatz,
Das Spätzlein,
Urda von Deutschland
Yours faithfully, loyally respectfully,
Mrs. Antonia U. Roberts
in the United Kingdom

21 February 2014, Friday, 0440

His Eminence Cardinal Vincent Nichols,
Westminster Cathedral,
Victoria Street, London SW1

The Fulfillment Of The Prophecy Of Our Lady Of Fatima For World Peace

Your Eminence Cardinal Nichols !
Dear Cardinal Nichols !

    Through the grace of the Infant Jesus of Prague and His Holy Mother Mary, I pray God to bestow on Thee His further Blessings, Love and Subjective Guidance in matters and issues of the Church.

I won't touch on Objective Issues because I am not the proper individual to comment on them. I would go direct to the point of my EX CATHEDRA Doctrine of the ONE SUPREME BEARER, in Whom Everything is contained and Who sustains Everything, the Mightiest and the most Supreme of Them and of Us All, Who has both Divine Nature and Human Nature, Whose Divine Nature and Divine Love has borne through all eternity, Almighty God the Father, our Creator, God the Son, our Redeemer Jesus Christ, God the Holy Spirit our Sanctificator; Whose Human Nature and Human Love has borne through all Eternity, the Human Mischief, the Angel Bearer of Light, the Reconciled Angel Lucifer, all united in Oneness with one another. In union with the Church Triumphant, the Church Militant and theChurch Sufferings. For the Oneness of Divine Nature and Human Nature, for the coming of God's Kingdom into this World, for the Peaceful Destiny of Humanity and for the solution to the Mystery of Life Everlasting. Forever And Ever. Amen. I am currently reviewing and rewriting my novel on this EX CATHEDRA Doctrine.

I enclose herewith some copies of my correspondences to the Popes, Her Royal Majesty, The Queen and other personages relevant to this Subjective Issue. I also enclose a copy of my autobiography, Schizo-Whispers. And other small booklets which I bought and picked up from the German Hospital in Nymphenburg, Munich, where I trained as a Nurse way back in 1963-1965. The course I didn't finish because I wanted to study in the Ludwig's-Maximillian's Universitaet in Muenchen.

I started writing to the Popes, in 1970, Pope Paul VI. I started receiving acknowledgements in 1981 from His Holiness Pope John Paul 11, of which I have had around six letters of unofficial acknowledgements, inclusive of two Papal Blessings In Absentia. Two replies from Pope Benedict XVI, inclusive of two coloured holy pictures of the Holy Family, but none from Pope Francis 1.

Also enclosed are recent copies of some short acknowledgements from whom I have sent my autobiography and my EX CATHEDRA Prayers. I had a Filipino Spiritual Director, Archbishop Onesimo Gordoncillo of Capiz, Roxas City, Philippines for when I had my Post-natal depression in the eighties. Since 1986. Previous to that, my Uncle, Bishop Epifanio B. Surban of the Diocese of Dumaguete, Negros Oriental in the Philippines was my spiritual Counsellor and Guidance. Mons. Onie passed away in December 2013.

Thine in the One Supreme Bearer, in Oneness with Almighty God the Father, our Creator, God the Son our Redeemer Jesus Christ, God the Holy Spirit our Sanctificator. And the reconciled Angel Bearer of Light, Angel Lucifer all united in Oneness with One Another. In union with the Church Triumphant, the Church Militant and the Church Sufferings. For the Oneness of Divine Nature and Human Nature, for the coming of God's Kingdom into this World, for the Peaceful Destiny of Humanity and for the Solution to the Mystery of Life Everlasting. Amen.

Prinzessin Urduja A. De Talion

Yours Humourfully, Das Kleine Spatzlein,

Urda von Deutschland

Yours respectfully, loyally, fraternally and humbly,

Mrs. Antonia Urduja Roberts of the UK

ARCHDIOCESE OF CAPIZ
CHANCERY OFFICE
P.O. Box 44 Roxas City—5800
Philippines

12 NOVEMBER 1995

DEAR ANTONIA U. T. ROBERTS & FAMILY,

WITH THIS I MOST SINCERELY THANK YOU FOR THE KIND LETTER/PHOTOS AND FAMILY NEWS. YOU HAVE BEEN ALWAYS MOST THOUGHTFUL! FOR THIS GOD BLESS YOU MOST ABUNDANTLY.
TL
THIS MONTH AND ONWARD I WILL BE DOING MY PASTORAL VISITATION BEGINNING WITH THE VICARIATE OF ST. GEMMA PARISHES. THIS IS ALWAYS A GOOD OPPORTUNITY FOR ME TO MEET THE FAITHFUL OF THE ARCHDIOCESE AS I REMIND THEM ABOUT GOD'S LOVE AND CONTINUED PROTECTION.

I WILL ALSO HAVE THE CHANCE TO ASK THE PEOPLE TO PRAY FOR AND TO CONTRIBUTE TO CONSTRUCTION OF OUR NEW COLLEGE SEMINARY WHICH THE HOLY SEE INSTRUCTED US TO BEGIN. PLEASE PRAY FOR THIS INTENTION.

REST ASSURED OF MY CONTINUED PRAYERS THAT GOD SHOWER UPON YOU AND YOUR LOVED ONES HIS CHOICEST BLESSINGS AND GRACES.

IN THE LOVE OF JESUS AND MARY,

Mons. Onie

ARCHDIOCESE OF CAPIZ
City of Roxas
Philippines
5800

Nº 1546

Date NOV. 4, 19 97

Received from *Antonia Roberts*
the amount of *Five Thousand Three Hundred Seventy-Six*
(₱ 5,376.10) as donation for the construction of the College Seminary of the Archdiocese of Capiz.

Thank you very much for your kindness and generosity. May our Lord reward you a hundredfold.

PNB check
m. 48593

Received by:

Oeconomus

ARCHDIOCESE OF CAPIZ
CHANCERY OFFICE, TEL. 211-053, ROXAS CITY, PHILIPPINES - 5800

5 November 1997

Dear Antonia T. Roberts,

Thank you most sincerely for the kind letter with the photos and the thoughtfulness in sending me you generous aid for the construction of our new Seminary College. This thoughtfulness of yours, I am sure, will be rewarded by the Lord most abundantly with His graces and abiding presence.

November is the month of Christ the King. It is very wholesome to think that inspite of all our woes in this world and of our own problems and trials, we form a part of Christ's Kingdom of love and peace with His interior presence in our hearts, in our communities and Christian families. We start to enjoy our Kings presence here on earth and yet we look forward to our heavenly abode. This is a consoling thought that stirs inside us as we continue our pilgrim way towards the great Jubilee Year 2000.

May the blessings of Jesus, who deigned to be one of us (whose Birthday we celebrate comes December), be showered upon you and the caring protection of the Blessed Mother be always extended on you and all your loved ones.

Warm regards... and God bless you.

In the Love of Jesus,

Mons. Onie

Mons. ONESIMO C. GORDONCILLO

5th September 2005

Dear Mons. Onie !

I hope you are well and fine.

I am sending you separately two copies of our church magazine, entitled The Echo. But I will ask the post office to attach this letter to the envelope for the magazines, so that you will receive both at the same time.

I am presently studying in The Open University, in Milton Keynes, England for about two years now. At present, I am taking a course entitled, Biological Psychology, Exploring the Brain and the Nervous System which I hope to finish this October 2005. One of the courses I would be taking in February next year is entitled, Religion Today: Tradition, Modernity and Change. This venture of mine has been one of the main channels that have improved my inner being, giving me peace and understanding in my mind and intellect and strengthening my relationships, inside and outside. I am doing a degree studies.

Familywise, Elsie, my daughter is now 28 years old and Seve, my son is now 23 years old. They have both finished their university studies and they both don't live at home anymore; therefore, its only Alan, my husband and myself living at home. Alan is also always busy with his own church.I am also very busy juggling my job, churches' activities, social activities,domestic duties and leisure. I have reached retiring age since last year, but I still work part-time. I feel that it is also therapeutic for me to go to work because it helps to put me in touch with outside realities, although I do believe that reality, in this ultra-modern, highly-developed technological world, is a relative matter and is a very confusingly-elusive phenomenon. And, I am very grateful for the prayers and spiritual support you have given me in the past when I was in dire need of them. Thank you ever so very much, in the name of Baby Jesus and Mother Mary.

I pray good health and long-healthy-life for your goodself and may Jesus and Mother Mary guide you always.

Respectfully and affectionately,

Antonia Urduja/Urda

Jersey City Medical Center
50 Baldwin Avenue
Jersey City, New Jersey 07304
United States of America

May 7, 1995

Dear Alan & Urding,

I should have written earlier as this is an acknowledgement of receipt of your letters I received a few weeks ago. At any rate, I'm very thankful for your invitation to stay with you the next time I visit England. I hope I could make it in the near future.

The news about how things are going here are not quite good. The bombing of the Federal Building in Oklahoma City was terrible, indeed. After so many days, they didn't expect to find any survivors in the rubble, so they decided to stop the search. The building was now totally demolished. Everybody here from the president to the people in the streets is outraged. There was no reason for it. Except for one who is not talking at all, all the other suspects are still at large. There's a massive manhunt for them going on all over the States. They can hide but sooner or later they will be found, no doubt about that. Meanwhile, the whole country grieves for those who lost their lives in this senseless ct of terrorism.

We are trying to get a US visa for Cito, Oking and Roger. Except for Roger, they already have their passports. But what is more difficult to get is the visa. We are hoping that because they have their families in the Philippines and they are somewhat advanced in age, the US Consulate will consider this. If they could make it here, it will be some celebration we will have on the occasion of Ma's 90th birthday. Much more so, if you all could come, which we deeply hope you would. Linda will surely come. She said so.

I got a good news about myself. It seems that I'm quite well now. My last lab work showed that my hemoglobin is now normal and my cholesterol has gone down quite considerably. My physician could hardly believe it, but that's what the results showed. There's no reason why we should suspect that the machines malfunctioned and gave a false information. Anyway, I'm still being closely monitored. In fact, this coming week I'll have another lab test.

Our governor, Christine Whitman Todd visited London recently. Before she left, she caused a commotion here in new Jersey. She made the statements to British journalists that Black teenagers here are competing as to who could impregnate the most before they get married. It's a terrible thing to say for foreign consumption but since she said it, there must some truth to it. By the way, she apologized.

With all the best, I am

Your cousin,

Jersey City Medical Center
50 Baldwin Avenue
Jersey City, New Jersey 07304
United States of America

February 19, 1998

Dear Urding,

I'm afraid I'll just have to be brief. My eye-sight is not yet back after a surgery. In fact, the doctor told me to stay away from computer as much as possible. Since coming back from the Philippines last July, I stopped driving. It may take a while before I could sit behind the wheel.

I received your nice letter, and let all the others read it. Sure, you can stay with us whenever you come. You and your family are always welcome. Some of us might be going home in July. Pining, Din and our nephew, Fr. Denis, are going to Rome. They are leaving this coming Saturday. I understand Linda will meet them in Rome. I don't know if they'll be going to Switzerland also.

Did you know that Tatang Ering passed away recently? Yes, he did after a long lingering illness. Tatang David, his brother, was home then on vacation. His daughter Judith who works here in New York, was not able to go home. Everybody else back home I suppose is doing well.

Regards to Alan, Elsie and Seve.

Your cousin,

Manoy Kuntic

JERSEY CITY MEDICAL CENTER

BALDWIN AVENUE   JERSEY CITY, NJ 07304   201 915 2000

May 13, 1998

Dear Urding,

Many thanks for the nice letter and the enclosed pictures. I shared them with the folks in Highland avenue. While in Calolbon last year, we enjoyed the frequent afternoon visit of Tatang Freding. Most often we reminisced the good old days, like probably we did of our days in Munich. Thank God for giving us such opportunity to share our joy with others. They made us happy and, hopefully, we made them happy as well.

We all have our long vacation planned already. Ruben left for Manila yesterday. His friend drove him to JFK International airport. The rest of us are going in July on different dates. I'm tentatively scheduled to leave on the first day of July but it remains doubtful now. Last week my right eye bled causing to lose its vision. The good news about it is that there's no detachment of the retina which the doctor was at first concerned about. There's a massive bleeding behind the eye. The doctor said it will clear up in time. However, if it doesn't in two weeks he has to drain the blood. I wanted him to assure me that I could go ahead with my vacation as planned. He said it depends on how it progresses.

Weather here, I believe, is not any better than yours over there. The cold lingers on. However we in this part of the country are a lot luckier than in most. Some States are flooded, others, especially in the southern part, are hit by strong tornadoes killing tens of people and leaving hundreds homeless. For three days, it has been continuously raining here, and it was just yesterday afternoon that the sun came out. Some people are happy about this because they say they don't have to worry about water shortage when hot weather comes.

If you go to attend the wedding of Jojo, Imelda's second son, as I heard you are planning, we'll see each other again in November. I'll do the wedding, and most of the clans are also going including Boy Anselmo, Nancy's brother who works in Miami, Florida. I'm sure you still remember him. He was with us in our excursion in Lawag.

It seems that we'll have Joseph Estrada for president. As you know, he was a popular movie actor who doesn't know much about running the government. He speaks English very poorly. But people idolize him simply because he was an actor. The election was held last Monday, May 11, and early returns have him way ahead of all the other ten candidates for president. He loves to compare himself with President Regan who, like him, was an actor before he became a politician and eventually as president of the United States. Estrada is encouraged by the fact that Regan was regarded as a good president. He said that if Regan proved to be a good president, he doesn't see any reason why he could not. A very faulty logic but that's what he says. Facts about himself don't seem to back

A Member of Liberty HealthCare System

up his contention. His election may not prove good for the Catholic Church. He was very strongly opposed by the Catholic hierarchy for, among other things, being womanizer, drunkard, gambler and inept. And to make it even worse, he was backed up by the Iglesia ni Kristo which, as you know, is very anti-Catholic.

Speaking of election, we had two candidates from our family. Oking, my older brother, and Boy, Mila's brother, ran for councilor in our town from opposing parties. We don't know yet if they won or lost. Aguat, our former mayor, won as vice-mayor running as an independent candidate. Dr. Romano was reelected mayor, a post he held for the past 20 years.

So long for now. Regards to all.

Your cousin,

Fr. Edmundo A. Surban

JERSEY CITY MEDICAL CENTER
BALDWIN AVENUE   JERSEY CITY, NJ 07304   201 915 2000

September 11, 1998

Dear Urding,

I hope you'll receive this before you and Alan leave for the Philippines I received your letter with the inserts a couple of days ago. I wish you a happy and safe trip. And may you enjoy your stay in Calolbon.

Elsie and her friend are welcome to stay in our house. I'll tell Yvone, our niece and caretaker, about this. Since it will be in November, there should be a constant supply of water being rainy season. In summer, our water system is almost always dry.

You mentioned the mansion of the Alcantaras in Marilima. Sure it's imposing. The weekends before I left, Sol organized a picnic for the clans. It was well attended, although quite a few didn't come. We met ex-governor Alcantara and his wife. They were very accommodating. We were told that our group was the first one to hold a picnic having been just recently opened to the public. In fact, the canteen was still under construction. It should be finished by the time Elsie and her friend go there.

Good luck and enjoy your holidays.

Your cousin,

Manay Nunting

Antonia Roberts

From:
To:
Sent:
Subject: Thank you

Urding,

Instead of clicking the reply to your email, I'm using your email address to see if it gets through. You see, in my email addresses I have three different of yours. I hope that this one is the right one.

Thank you for the abbreviated biography of Alan. I admire him for his services to his country. I'm sure the British government is aware of this and give him his due. To serve one's country in the military is a noble thing to do. Remember Tata Eping? He entered the service as a young priest and the war caught up with him. He was in Bataan at the height of the war, and eventually joined in the Death March with thousands of other captive soldiers from Bataan to Sto. Tomas in Manila. Thank God he was one of the few who survived the infamous ordeal. I myself tried going to the US army although I was already overaged then. I passed all interviews and I thought I was already taken in. But when the result of the physical came, I failed because of my diabetis. I would have been assigned in Germany as my choice.

It's important to abide by the decision of doctors regarding our health. If they prescribe medication, we should take it religiously. We had one priest in Dumaguete who was quite important in the ministry who stopped taking his medication. Young as he was, he died. In my case, I have had different medications. At one time I was taking 12 pills one of them was as big as half an inch in diameter. It made my throat sore. When it became dificult for me, I suggested to the doctor to give me a shot instead. Fortunately, she agreed. Yesterday I went for my physical check-up. Since my diabetis goes up and down quite drastically, she recommended a different kind of insulin. I hope it will work better than the one I presently use.

Did I tell you that Pininay (Pining) fell down the stariways and hurt herself bad? Yes, she did a week ago. She couldn't remember how she fell but we figure out that she did head first. There's a slight bleeding in the brain and a broken bone in the neck but the doctor said that there's nothing exciting about them because they will heal by themselves. In addition she got a broken check bone that affects a little her eyesight. The worse is her damage in the wrist. Yesterday she had a surgery. There are pins that go through her wrist to repair the broken bones. She's still in pain. She will be placed in the rehab for further therapeutic measures.

Ruben left the other day for Manila and at this time, he's just arriving in Virac. His flight to Virac was cancelled because of rain and he was forced to check in a hotel to wait for the flight the next day. I told Imelda about your book and she said you promised to send her a copy.

Regards and stay well.

Antonia Roberts

From:
To:
Sent:
Subject: Re: Thank you

Dear Manoy Munding,

Yes, I received your Email dated 14 May 2008, 16:20. My   is my best email address.   also works but I seldom visit this program.   is already non-existent. Thank you for your above email. Such a pleasant feeling I felt as I read your messages. It was a good read. Yes, I have sent Giliw a book.

And another yes...I haven't forgotten about Tata Epings joining the Death March from Bataan to Sto. Tomas, Manila. I have a lot to be thankful for to Tata Eping; he was very good to me. He even married Alan and I in the Catholic church in March 22,1985, on our 11th civil wedding anniversary. He also baptized Seve at the age of 3 years in Dumaguete. Cesing and Nanang Tinay were our two sponsors at our wedding. He pampered Alan. It was he who advised me to keep in touch with my cousins and other relatives in various parts of the world. Its a shame that you failed being accepted in the US Army because of your diabetes.

I didn't know what got into the mind of Alan, why he started not taking his insulin and his other medications and not eating proper food. I wasn't completely aware of all these because I never used to check him since I trusted him fully. Perhaps, I'd been shortsighted. Funny enough, for one month before these episodes, I also withdrew from taking one of my tablets. I felt good and I wanted to discontinue it for good. But all I did was pray, ate as little as possible and existed on water. But eventually, the memories of one of my friends from the Catholic church kept recurring into my mind. His name was John- he was tall, white, blond and handsome and I had a 'crush' on him. He was a wing-commander in the RAF (Royal Air Force) and was assigned in Germany and in Japan during the war. He was very active in church activities because he was retired. I even composed a German poem for him, one Christmas and we used to joke and laugh , Urda's sense of humour, in church. He would curtsy to me on occasions and he enjoyed our laughters. Then, I just noticed that he didn't go to the Silver Circle Club anymore. I saw him once on a Sunday morning in church and he was walking with a stick/cane. I went to him after the mass and he said he was fine. He has stopped taking his tablets- he told me. A few weeks after that, I heard that he was confined in a nursing home. Some few weeks afterwards, I saw him again in the church and he was on a wheelchair being pushed by another parishioner. That was the last time I saw him alive. Not long after that, I read in the parish newsletter about his death and funeral. I told my doctor about my one-month withdrawal from one of my tablets and related to her John's story. I really got frightened- I told myself that I didn't want to be dead yet and become a saint so soon; I've still got so many things to do here in this world.I did a self-rehab.

I'm sorry to hear about Pining's fall, down the stairways. I shall think of her in my prayers and send her some healing thoughts and prayers. I'll tell you something that happened to me. In 1981, it was my second day at home after having given birth to Seve and discharged from hospital, I was having a bath. Then I stood up and right after stepping out of the bath, I fell on the bathroom floor and became unconscious. Alan was not at home and the bathroom door was locked. I must have been unconscious on the floor for about 5 or 10 minutes. When I became conscious, I was very thankful that I was on the floor ! Suppose, I got unconscious in the bath... I would have been drowned ! Frightening....It still occasionally haunts me.

My brother, Geny in Canada, advised me to send a copy of my book with an accompanying letter to the Oprah Winfre Show in Chicago. I'll let you know if something comes out of this.

Wie Mutti Elia, unserer Deutschen Mutti, viele herzliche gruesse und Gottes segen.

Urda

Antonia Roberts

From:
To:
Sent:
Subject:

Urding,

Pining and I are grateful for your eCard. Thank you for your inspiring thoughts. Pining is now walking around but every now and then she feels pain in her back. She can't go back to work becau there are still pins in her arms. We encourage her to just retire after all she's already of retirement age. She loves to work and she hates to stop working. As I told you, I had appointment with my ey doctor. He was pleased by the improvement the eye drop works on it. I don't have to go through ey surgery, thank God.

Just yesterday I finished reading the book. It invokes a lot of fond memories of my days in Munich didn't know that you moved from one work to another that many times. And it seems easy to get employment at the time. I wonder if it's still the same today. I'm wondering why Schw. Elia didn't want you to see you when you went to Germany for vacation. You didn't mention her anymore sinc then and I'm wondering too if you saw her again. I remember one incident where Gernot was involved. In fact, he was the one who invited us for lunch. I'm not sure if you were with us, but Cesing, Imelda and Donna were. Before leaving the hospital, Schw. Elia told me to limit the expenses because Gernot was just a medical student and that he didn't have much money. When the bill was presented, I grabbed it. Gernot didn't like it but I insisted that I pay the bill.

I envy you for being able to travel far and wide. You have seen a lot of Europe and I like to believe that you'll see a lot more in the future. I wish I could do likewise. But age and deteriorating health had caught up with me. I could'nt even walk a short distance without taking a rest. I could have gon with Ben (he's due back on Saturday) to Calolbon but I was afraid of what might happen to me whil there. Perhaps it's a baseless fear but it's fear just the same. I notice over the years that bad health occurs without warning. And if it does, I should be able to reach my doctor immediately. Hospitals in the Philippines are expensive. My health insurance doesn't cover hospitalization outside the United States. In St. Luke's Medical Center where I was admitted last summer, every little thing the use on you has a price. A cotton swab costs P5.00. Even the splint is paid. I had syrenges for my insulin but if it happened that they accidentally used theirs, they would replace it with my own. It's rediculous but that's how it is over there.

Say hello to Alan, Elsie and Seve. I wish them the best of health.

Regards.

Antonia Roberts

From:
To:
Sent:
Subject:

Urding,

I haven't received the card yet. Before anything else, say happy birthday for me to Alan. At 71, he's still a young man. I'm now approaching 74 and still I think I'm young. Although I may look old on account of my serious illnesses, I would insist that at that age I'm still far from being an old man. Don't you think so?

Family reunion is a good thing to hold. You get in touch with your relatives which is seldom practice nowadays. People are so busy that they don't have time to get together with relatives. They become somewhat isolitionists, that's the right word. Imagine people in the apartments. They don't even know their next door neighbor let alone talk to one another. When parents are place in the nursing home, some children seldom if ever go to visit them. There's this classic thought: how come parents are able to take good care of ten children but ten children can't take care of one parent.

The other Sunday we visited Tatang David in the rehab. All of us from Highland plus Ponching and Fr. Denis. As you know, Tatang David has lost his mind/ Senile might be the right word. He still can recognize a little bit, but he doesn't talk. He just stares at you. I'm wondering why is this happening to our clan, Tatang Ering, Nanang Trining and unfortunately Tatang Freding, and of course our lolas before them. Remember Tilalay, Lola Taling and Lola Epay? They all ended up the same. Going back to our visit with Tatang David, being a Sunday Denis and I said Mass for the community. I didn't think that that many would attend, so I brought a limited number of hosts. It was not enough. Tatang David received communion.

Since we settled in the US, Dodo and I met only twice. Once in the late 70s when he was still priest, I visited him in the church he was serving. Then in the 80s, we met in his friends house close to the hospital I was working in. That was it. He told me to call him anytime so we could have lunch together. I never did. Dodo happened to be my close friend when we were studying in Rome. We took the bus together, took snacks together and sat gother in the classroom. Here's his address: Mr. Toribio Villacastin, 150-15 Barclay Avenue, Flushing, New York, 11355. This is his address in the 80s. I hope he's still there. I'm sure he would be glad to hear from you, espcially if you send him your book.

Regards.

Antonia Roberts

From:
To:
Sent:
Subject: keeping-up with family history

Dear Manoy Munding,

Thank you for wishing Alan Happy Birthday. He was pleased that you still remember him. In fact, he wrote a few words in the postcard I sent to you. Alan does not feel old; I also don't feel old, I always feel like "Nene" that little girl of Tatay and Nanay..."You are as young as you feel..." they always say.

Thank you, too, for your recent E-mail and the whereabouts of Dodo Villacastin. I will write to him first without sending him the book and I will see how it goes from there.

I'm sorry to hear about Tatand David in the rehab. He must be in his eighties by now. The last time I heard about him was when he had an operation and was in crutches. I send him a get-well card and his wife wrote to me with an enclosed photograph of herself holding their baby. I think that was decades ago. I replied to that letter and never got anymore reply until now. Anyway, I don't know what happened to that letter.

Yesterday (19/8/08) one of our residents celebrated her 100th birthday ! She still walks with or without a stick sometimes and she is not senile!! She has a certain sense of humour which makes her an endearing soul. I sing to her sometimes at nights before sleeping and we have developed a certain rapport. She occasionally gets depressed but she reads newspapers and books, especially autobiographies. However, she has a pacemaker. We have another resident who is 95 years old. She has had a mild heart attack around Christmas last year before transferring to our Home. She adorns herself with sets of jewellry, like me, and she is also not senile. She loves letter writing and likes to talk. She sometimes behaves like a teenager. She reads newspapers. Both of them do their personal care by themselves with as little help as possible from the carers She walks very well on her own like a youngster.. She, too, is not senile. Another resident who is also not senile is an 87 year old lady, but she is very fat and walks with a zimmer-frame. However, she suffers from cystitis of the kidney, She reads a lot, too, newspapers, murder-mystery books by Dick Francis and a few others, watches television and devours crosswords. She is practically dependent upon the carers for her personal care. The other 6 residents are in some stages of senile dementia. " They've lost their minds to the fairies", we usually say.

Tatay had Alzheimers, I was told. He had 3 major operations. Manay Ester Alcantara, the wife of my millionaire cousin, Manoy Beroy, who was Governor of Catanduanes for a while (I am not boasting, I am using Tatay's style of voicing out his style of writing and his thoughts, as we had symbiotic learning styles) told me secretly in 1978 , during our first trip to Manila with Alan and two year old Elsie, that Tatay was born with an ingrained cyst in his lungs which was benign and which didn't grow. He had an operation in 1972 in the Chinese General Hospital to take out this cyst but the surgeon decided to leave it alone as it was benign. It would be more serious to get rid of it. Then he had two more major operations in St. Lukes with his bladder. He was with us here in England, I think, it was in 1982, when Ninoy Aquino was assassinated as he came down the airplane. He saw it happen live on television and he was very worried. Instead of staying in England for a year as was his visa and airticket, he only stayed from July until the day after my September 18th birthday, a day before yours, in 1982. He was confined overnight in the out-patient hospital here and rejected the offer to have an operation here to take off his kidney stone which would have been November 1982. Not long after he arrived back in the Philippines, he had an operation in St. Lukes in Quezon City. My youngest sister, Tita Talion works in St. Lukes for over a decade now. She's now the acting manager of the Electrocardiogram department.I advised her not to leave St. Luke's because the family gets percentage off for their hospitalization. St. Lukes is the best and largest chest hospital in the Far East, I was told.

Tatay made it his personal responsibility that I didn't get alienated from my family, so ever since I went to Munich in 1963 at age 17 years old, he wrote to me as often as possible(we were so far yet so very near to each other like one person) We used to argue and quarrel in our letters and he used to reprimand me and would write to me his moral and spiritual issues and beliefs, sent me stories of what's happening to family members, send me photographs and so on and so forth. That was why, while I was becoming Europeanized in my mentality and personality, I was watching my brothers and sisters in my heart and in my mind, grow-up from a distance---so far and yet so very near. Tata Eping said that I had had so much...that I've exceeded my mental and emotional limitations, that's why I had nervous breakdowns. Let alone, those Talion relatives of mine who looked up to me as a role model in their process of attaining their dreams....it wasn't and is isn't easy to be a 'role model' you have to live up to it. But it was and is fun and enjoyable, sometimes. That's why many celebrities end up in drugs !

I remember Lola Tilalay vividly. She didn't want to have a bath. And when she would smell and no one could bear it anymore, Lola Bay's maids would bath her. She would refuse and fight and swear when being bathed and then she would run and walk to Lola Quicay's house, our house. Then our maids would finish her off with extra swearings from her. All is peaceful for a period of time staying at our house until she started to smell again. I can remember vividly at mealtimes, when I would sometimes sit next to her. Her head had loads of lice creeping up and down her hair...! Then they would persuade her to bath and there's refusing and fighting and swearing and running and walking wet, to Lola Bay's house and so on and so forth. Lola Tilalay used to stereotypically chant, "Tararantantang !!!" as often as possible !!!Have you noticed that then? I don't know about Lola Anna, Lola Talin, Lola Epay, Tatang Ering and Nanag Trining. I don't know if Lola Quicay ever got senile. When I left Calolbon in July 1963, that was the last time I saw her. She was always very clean and orderly and always had a piece of cloth hanging on the belt of her 'tapis' together with her keys, to wipe the tables whenever she felt like doing it. I remember during fiestas, our long table would already have all the guest sitting around it, even Lolo would be on the other end of the table. Lola's place was at the other end of the long table which was vacant. Then she would enter the dining room, she would start to undo her tapis, and put is all over again. Then she would undo her hair-bun and would comb and bun it all over again while everyone was waiting for her to sit. Then, she would spit once or twice on the floor just before she sat on the table. Like a reina de las flores! Tatay would laugh it out but everyone was silently watching her. I think she died in May 1964, while I was already in Krankenhaus. I remember receiving Tatay's letter with the news of her death. I immediately went to one of the guest rooms in the nurses' home and I really cried my heart's out, all alone. I wanted to be alone in my grief.

Alan is off to Kettering, about 40 miles from home, to lecture on Healing in one of his churches. He is also a distant learning tutor in Spiritual Healing and he uses the Email with some of his students. Its good for him to be busy. He enjoys his work, therefore, it keeps him happy and pleased , although it could be exhausting mentally, sometimes.Most of his students are women, therefore, it keeps his ego well fed. I tolerate his contacts with the feminine homo sapiens, and I don't get jealous about it. I know my side of the bargain.His work is voluntary, although he gets refund for his expenses. Received a letter from Cesing. But, I'll mention it next time.

Best wishes and Kind regards,

Affectionately,

Urding/Urda/Antonia/Tonie

Prinzessin Uduja A. de Talion
World Peace TASK
MABUHAY · Import-Export

3rd September 2005

Hi Fr. Tim !

Update of the Fulfillment of the Prophecy of Our Lady of Fatima for World Peace

I have several enclosures with this letter. A few photocopies of the letters of acknowledgement from various personages. I must have had about ten replies from the Vatican, one of them had my reference number in the archives of the Vatican where my many letters and personal articles which I've sent to them-photos, prayer books, a crucifix I bought in Munich in 1963 which I used to carry everywhere, an old, worn-out baby-shirt of mine, letters, poems and many other things, I've lost or misplaced those letters, and many other replies. I first wrote to Pope Paul VI in 1970, but the first reply I received from the Vatican was in 1981(?) from His Holiness Pope John Paul 11. When I had my post-natal depression and I had no regular job, I wrote and wrote and read and read and did so many things. I frequented the Westminster Cathedral and the Westminster Abbey then. Anyway, I won't delve so much in the past.

Now, let's deal with the present. My advertisement in The Echo would, I hope, activate the neurotransmitters in my brain to rechannel the spiritual energy which would be redirected for the issues on world peace. I am at present studying for a BA/BSc (Honours) Health and Social Care with The Open University for about two years now. I am just finishing a course on Biological Psychology this October 2005. In February 2006, one of the courses that I would be taking is entitled: Religion Today: Tradition, Modernity and Change, a 9 month course, Level 3, 60 points. I work 4 nights , 2 nights each in two nursing and residential homes. My 2 children are now 28 years old and 23 years old. Etc. etc.etc. I am writing you all these because I would like to occasionally consult you on this behalf(I would ask Fr. John details about you) if necessary. You as my English Spiritual Director. My Filipino Spiritual Director is Archbishop Onesimo Gordoncillo, Archdiocese of Capiz, Roxas City, Philippines. We still, occasionally correspond, but not as often as when I was ill with post-natal depression in the past. I used to escort him around Munich, West Germany in 1965 when he was still a priest reading for his Doctorate in Theology in the Colegio Seminario de Filipino in Rome, when he got invited a few times to the German Hospital run by the Friars and Nuns of St.Francis of Assisi, Third Order,where I was then training as a German nurse, and my uncle who was then a Bishop and was the Director of the Philippine Mission Society in the Philippines used to get invited to in that hospital.

I'm sorry, the contents of this letter are not properly and grammatically styled. But, I don't really have time to rearrange the grammatical style. I am giving you this pocket book of Lance Armstrong, which I hope you would enjoy. Thank you for everything and God bless you... Good luck, good health and God bless.

Sisterly your in Jesus and Mother Mary,

Antonia Roberts

Antonia Roberts

From:
Date:
To:
Cc:
Subject:

Dear Antonia,

Easter greetings to you. How nice it was to receive your letter recently and its contents. My apologies for taking so long to write. I had been in South Africa, Kenya and Ireland and only returned earlier this week. On my arrival your letter was awaiting me.

I was so happy to read the wonderful news and blessing for Clare and Seve. God is good and I pray that the remaining months before birth will be joyful and healthy.

I will write a card to you with my postal address, as you say you misplaced my last letter to you.

Thank you so much for your very generous contribution to the Mission of the Church. I may have explained to you that all Mass stipends I receive go towards school fees for children in Kenya. I have a number of children I sponsor and this will enhance their education and life.

Your Mass intentions will be offered - be assured of that.

I also ask you for prayers for my mother. She is gravely ill and close to death. She has terminal cancer and each day it takes a bit more of her. She is now very weak and recently also had a stroke. We are praying now just for peace of mind and to be pain free. I shall go home to her next Monday for at least a week. Throughout the summer, and indeed, the time that is remaining, I will go to Ireland often to be with her.

Antonia, I wish you well and look forward to meeting sometime.

Every blessing to you and your extended family. Thank you for your letter, your thoughtfulness and kindness,

Liam

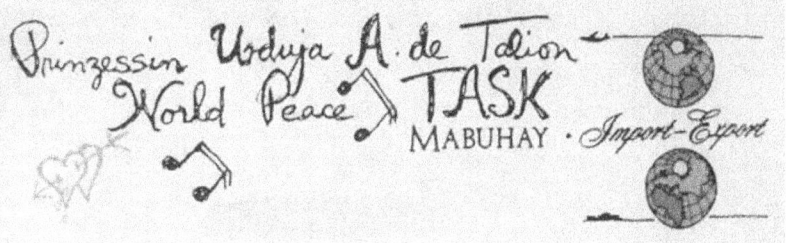

27 April 2009

Dear Fr. Webster,

I was inspired by your sermon yesterday during the 10-30 AM Holy Mass in the Our Lady Queen of Heaven Catholic Church. Thank you.

I enclose herewith two cheques totalling £150 = 00 for the Redemptorist Mission-Zimbabwe appeal; also enclosed is my first book which I hope would be followed by several more in the future.

Thank you again, and please think of me in your prayers, once in a while.

Sincerely yours,

Mrs. Antonia U. Roberts

31 December 2012-12-31

Rev. Mavis Wilson,
St. Peter's Church,
Frimley, Surrey

Dear Rev. Wilson,

My best wishes for the incoming year 2013 to you and yours.

I was just thinking that I thought it was thoughtless of me to just attend a service in St. Peter's after not having done so for years, without asking permission from you or yours. I am thinking of occasionally attending the 1030 AM Holy Comunion on Wednesdays, and maybe occasionally the Sunday Service at 1000 AM. I do normally attend the 0830 to 0930 AM Holy Mass on Sundays in the Our Lady Queen of Heaven on Sundays. I go to confession sometimes in Westminster Cathedral in London or sometimes in OLQH.

I was used to dealing with international sets of people of various nationalities, denominations, social and religious classes in my youth and I wish to understand how their mentalities operate for mutual understanding. Mutual understanding of mentalities can be a small pathway to world peace. These had already been done before lots of times, but the world is changing day by day, and year by year, so do our mental and emotional outlooks. After several upheavals in my life, I am continuing my Journey in Faith, Hope and Love, Alone but not alone…through the grace of the Godhead.

How is Rev. Barbara Clements? I keep her in my prayers. I did visit her on my own at least twice in the past but I was advised to have a companion should I visited her again. Since then, I lost track. It was Barbara who brought me to the World of St. Peters and friends in Frimley. I never regretted it. I don't know if Barbara is still alive, if so, if she still remembers me, please kiss her Happy New Year 2013 for me. Thanks.

I hope the good Lord showers you and yours with His abundant graces and a Joyous New Year 2013. Thank you for everything.

Yours sincerely,

15th June 2006

His Excellency
President George W. Bush,
The White House,
Washington D.C.
U. S. A.

Your Excellency
President Bush !

The Fulfillment Of The Prophecy Of Our Lady Of Fatima For World Peace

I pray that You are well and fine.

Such an old-fashioned title exudes an aroma of fragrant- blossoms and lightens the heavy burden of the President of a powerful nation such as that of the U. S. A. It reminds me of those days when I was a little girl and when my Father/Tatay took his oath in the presence of His Excellency President Elpidio Quirino of the Philippines, after passing the Bar. Those were the days......

Thank You for upholding the dignity and sanctity of marriage between a man and a woman.....

There is Joy in Forgiveness nurtured and strengthened by Love...

GOD BLESS AMERICA and HER PRESIDENT

HIS EXCELLENCY GEORGE W. BUSH !

THINE in the **ONE SUPREME BEARER**, in Whom Everything is contained and Who sustains Everything, the Mightiest and the most Supreme of Them and of Us All, Who has both Divine Nature and Human Nature, Whose Divine Nature and Divine Love borne Almighty God the Father, our Creator, God the Son, our Redeemer Jesus Christ, God the Holy Spirit our Sanctificator; Whose Human Nature and Human Love borne the Human Mischief, the Reconciled Angel Lucifer, all united in Oneness with One Another; in Union with the Church Triumphant, the Church Militant and the

Church Sufferings; for the Oneness of Divine Nature and Human Nature, for the coming of God's Kingdom into this World, for the Peaceful Destiny of Humanity and for the solution to the Mystery of Life Everlasting. Amen.

Prinzessin Urduja A. de Talion

Das Kleine und Humourvolle Spatzlein,

Urda von Deutschland

Yours respectfully, humbly and affectionately in Baby Jesus and Mother Mary,

Mrs. Antonia U. T. Roberts

Urding/ Urda/ Tonie

Herewith several enclosures :

Copies of my renewal letters, on behalf of this prophecy, to The Pope, The Queen, Archbishop O. Gordoncillo and to Fr. John O'Sullivan of the Parish of Our Lady Queen of Heaven, Catholic Church, Frimley, Surrey.

Other documents enclosed are- my EX CATHEDRA Prayer which was unofficially acknowledged and blessed by His Holiness Pope John Paul 11, my updated CV, a few of my Writings relevant to my studies with The Open University and a few simple, personal photographs.

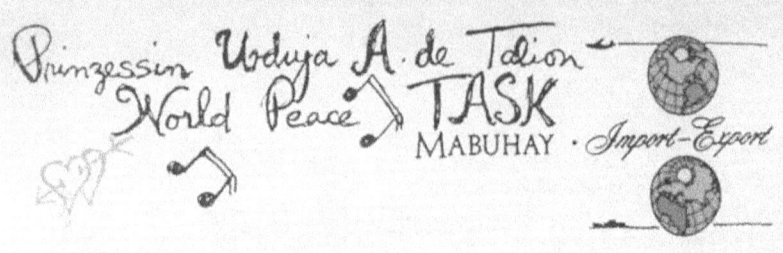

27 January 2009

President Barack H. Obama,
White house,
Washington D.C.,
U. S. A.

Your Excellency Pres. Obama,
Dear Sir,

    With "The Audacity Of Hope" for my World Peace Task, I approach Your Excellency with Humility in my Heart and Mind.

The issues of my Dreams cover Spiritual, Nerval, Emotional and Mental Health through Prayers, Immentalitation, Inculturation and Acculturation, the Quadriune God/Goddess of the One Supreme Bearer in Oneness with Almighty God the Father, our Creator, God the Son, our Redeemer Jesus Christ, God the Holy Spirit, our Sanctificator and the Human Mischief, the Reconciled Angel Bearer of Light, Angel Lucifer... All united in Oneness with one another, in Union with the Church Triumphant, the Church Militant and the Church Sufferings, for the Oneness of Divine Nature and Human Nature, for the coming of God's Kingdom into this World, for the Peaceful Destiny of Humanity and for the Solution to the Mystery of Life Everlasting forever and ever. Amen.

I enclose herewith my autobiography, which Humility aside and without being audacious, I hope your goodself would be able to read amidst your many duties. It would enable you to understand the essence and substance of my Ex Cathedra Doctrine of the Quadriune God/ Goddess, my Prayers relevant thereto are written at the end of the novel. Also enclosed is A Simple Prayer Book which I'd been praying since I was a young girl in the Philippines before I flew to Munich in Germany in 1963. Now, I pray all the prayers therein everyday for increase of Faith and Hope in God and for clarity of mind and thoughts. Perhaps, with the consent of Mrs. Michelle Obama and under her direction, I wish to give it as a gift to Malia and Sasha.

I just thought that, perhaps, you could try for a baby while in the White House. It could be a boy this time. Tony and Cherie Blair did it while in 10 Downing Street. How about you and Michelle?

I enjoyed reading your two books- Dreams Of My Father and The Audacity Of Hope- with joyous emphaty.

I also wrote about these Ex Cathedra Doctrine and Prayers to President Reagan, and President Bush(both Senior and Junior) while they were still in office. Although I've never received an acknowledgement from them, yet I was not disappointed nor discouraged.

I am a "One-Woman Band" " I am, yet I am not." " Alone yet not alone, but with Everyone in Spirit and in Hope for these Dreams for Peace. One of my main Anchors- Prayers can move Mountains." You and America are in my prayers, all the time.

My best wishes and prayers. God bless.

Prayerfully and respectfully yours,

Mrs. Antonia Urduja Talion Roberts

Excerpts And Snippets On My
 Self-Psychoananlysis, Self-Healing And Forgiveness
By Mrs. Antonia Urduja Talion Roberts

10 July 1995

His Excellency,
President Fidel Ramos,
Malacanyang Palace,
Metro Manila, Philippines

Your Excellency, President Ramos,

Re: Task For The Fulfillment Of The Prophecy Of Our Lady Of Fatima For World Peace

Issues:
1. EX CATHEDRA Creed/Doctrine of the Quadriune God/Goddess of the One Supreme Bearer.
2. The above EX CATHEDRA and other relevant matters that I have already written to the Vatican and to several other respectable personages in the past years are mentioned within the enclosed copy of my letter to Princess Diana, Prince Charles, Prime Minister John Major and Her Royal Majesty, The Queen.
3. In December 1992, I have suffered a very, very serious Nerve-setback due to circumstances borne out of misunderstandings, unawareness, misinterpretations of motivational factors allied to actions and decisions I have made whereby they had been judged in accordance with western eyes and have not been read through Filipino eyes. I have never crawled so hard on the ground and for a very great length of time, alone, having been judged unjustly. But as we say, God moves in mysterious ways. And I have used Positive Mental Attitude and spiritual optimism in sorting out and in understanding the individual-contradictions involved therein, as results of mentality differences which included so many different aspects of human nature(their subjectiveness and objectiveness.) I counted my blessings. I never realized that I had so many friends who had showered me with genuine love and affection without ulterior motivations, kindness, spiritual and moral support as guideposts in the Pathways I had had to tread- so as to be able to stand up straight again. " Alone- yet not alone." And I owe these beautiful friends of mine gratitude and affection in Jesus' name. Friends- yes, I am good in making friends; even when I was in Munich way back in 1963-1967, I also had so very many international and cosmopolitan friends in various categories. But I never actually counted them nor have I taken note of what I have shared myself with them.
4. And in times of need, they all resurface from my unconscious and I thank God for them because they give me the incentive and strength, to a greater or lesser degree, to carry on with my "interrupted pathways" for growth on behalf of the fulfilment of this Task for the Prophecy of Our Lady of Fatima for World Peace. The Growth I have achieved is tremendous and I wish to thank God for all my Friends- seen or unseen, visible and invisible- who I have leaned on at

certain times when I felt so very weak and I needed to rest, sometimes to cry on someone else's shoulders.
5. My beloved, mystical and beautiful Philippines, I have always and I always carry her within me…both within my mind and within my heart of hearts. I love her, oh, so very,very much and I know I would never have been able to do what I had to do without her- the Land of the Morning, the Land of the Sun Caressed!!! His Holiness Pope John Paul 11 knows about me and my Task.
6. Sister Renee Navato, who used to be the High School principal of St. Paul's College, Dumaguete City, Philippines where I was in First Year High School, years circa 1957-58 , entertained us when my family and I visited Dumaguete City way back in March 1985. My then uncle, Bishop Epifanio B. Surban, married my husband and myself in the Catholic church on our 11th Civil Wedding Anniversary. Sister Renee was then the Mother Superior of the whole St. Paul's College. She wrote to me and one of the thoughts she sent me was was Dr. Jose Rizal, our Philippine National Hero said that –
7. "A Filipino is like a molave tree,
8. It bends with the wind in stormy weather, left, right and centre and down below, but in the end, it always stands up straight. "
9. 6 – 30 pm   10 July 1995.

Yours respectfully,
Mrs. Antonia Urduja Talion Roberts
Das Spatzlein, Urda von Deutschland
Princess Urduja A. de Talion

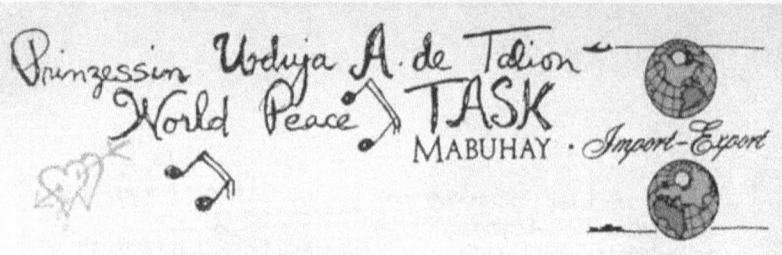

His Excellency
President Fidel Ramos,
Malacanyang Palace,
Manila, Philippines

Dear President Ramos,

Re: Task For The Fulfillment Of The Prophecy Of Our Lady Of Fatima For

WORLD PEACE !

Please allow me to show my respects with a firm and gentle friendly handshake. I have written to you about this Prophecy of Our Lady of Fatima in late 1992. Before that, I've written to Ex-President Cory Aquino. This time, I express my wishes, views and requests through the enclosed letters herewith.

They are from....Archbishop Onesimo Gordoncillo of Capiz who is my Filipino Spiritual Director. And the others are for, my cousin, Governor Severo Alcantara of Catanduanes, Senator Francisco Tatad, Ian Linden the General Secretary of the Catholic Institute for International Relations, Cardinal Basil Hume, His Royal Highness Prince Charles and Her Royal Majesty Queen Elizabeth 11. I also enclose copy of my EX CATHEDRA Prayers, my version of Rudyard Kipling's Ballads of East and West and the Catanduanes Anthem.

I am grateful for the attention that your excellency will give to these matters about the Prophecy for World Peace. May the good God guide you always

THINE in the One Supreme Bearer/Bathala...........

Princess Urduja A. de Talion
Yours good-humouredly, The Little Birdie, Das kleine Spatz,
Das Spatzlein,
Urda von Deutschland
Yours respectfully, faithfully, and sincerely,
Mrs. Antonia Urduja Roberts
of the United Kingdom

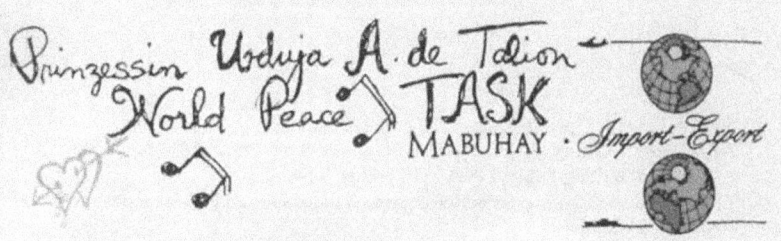

Dr. Jane Norris-Hill,
Marketing & Recruitment Manager,
University of Wales, Lampeter
Lampeter, Ceredigion
SA48 7ED

Dear Dr. Norris-Hill,

Thank you for the very interesting brochure of the university which you've sent me.

I am specially interested in the Taught Masters degree- hopefully to qualify for an MA/MTh of the University of Wales. I need to find out more of the methodology and other relevant matters for my research on mental health allied to religious experiences, mentalities, transubstantiation, vision, feelings, emotions, nerves....

I have a BA degree in the University of Sto. Tomas, Manila, Philippines, the oldest Catholic University in the Far East, in 1963. I have studied and trained in a Nursing course in a German Hospital- Krankenhaus des Dritten Orden in Munich, West Germany in 1963- 1965, in the German language. I have also studied Germanistik for two years in the Ludwig-Maximillian's Universitaet in Munich, West Germany in 1965- 1967. But, I was not able to finish this because I was taken ill and had had to go back to the Philippines in 1967. I was back in London in July 1969. I was previously in London in 1964-1965 for six months.

I am currently studying in the Open University to qualify for a BSc (Honours) Health and Social Care. Herewith below are some of my courses, their levels, duration and points gained:

K100 – Understanding Health and Social Care, Level 1, 60 points, a Certificate Course which I've passed. A foundation course for Health Studies. This qualified me as an OU Alumnus. 9 months

SD226 – Biological Psychology: Exploring the Brain and the Nervous System, Level 2, 60 points, 9 months

NVQ Level 3- Health and Social Care and NVQ Level 4 – Managing Care- accredited by the OU with 60 points through Credit Transfer. A year.

Y152 – Level 1, Open to Change, 10 points, 3 months
A174 – Start Writing Fiction: Level 1, 10 points, 3 months
A172- Start Writing Essay, Level 1, 10 points, 3 months
T185-Practical Thinking, an online course on metaphors and life experiences, Level 1, 10 points, 3 months.

Currently, I am taking 2 courses to finish in October 2006.
AD317 – Religion Today: Tradition, Modernity and Change, Level 3, 60 points, 9 months

A215 – Creative Writing, Level 2, 6o points, 9 months

I am Filipina by birth and am married to an Englishman for 32 years, with two grown-up children of 28 years and 23 years, who are both university graduates. I aim to take advantage of distance-learning with occasional visits to the university to confer with my tutors, use the library, attend seminars and lectures, meet fellow-colleagues and enjoy the environment in Lampeter. I shall appreciate it if you can send me details of this taught degree to start in 2007, the modules, duration, fees and the methods of payment and other necessary information. Please send me an application pack, also.

Thank you.

Yours sincerely,

Mrs. Antonia Urduja Talion Roberts

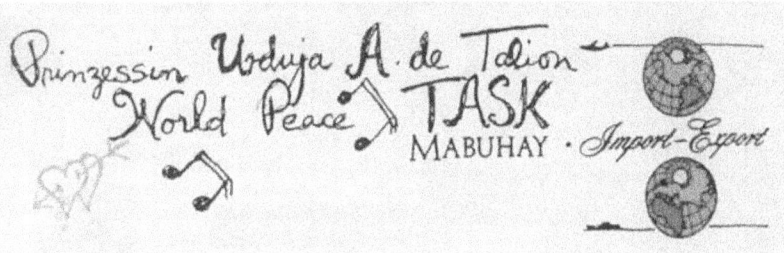

For The Fulfillment Of The Prophecy Of Our Lady Of Fatima For World Peace

Thank you ever so much for the wonderful, adorable and handsome and beautiful Doctors, Nurses and Carers, who helped in one way or another in the decompression of my right shoulder.

It was like travelling heavenwards with the Saints and Angels in Heaven. I peeped inside, curious to see what it was like, but St. Peter told me that I was not allowed there just yet. I need to go back to the World for I have lots more things to do for World Peace. How? I have no idea, how.

Herewith enclosed are a few of my two published books relevant thereto. I am at present compiling my written materials, hoping to be published by next year. Echoes Of My Mind- that would be the title. Herewith are some photocopies of some of the letters of acknowledgement on behalf of my books.

Hope you'll enjoy eating my chocolates.

Again, thank you so very much for all your kindness, beauty and skills, and practically for everything you've done for me. God bless you All.

Mrs. Antonia Urduja Roberts
24/09/2014

Prinzessin Usduja A. de Tdion
World Peace **TASK**
MABUHAY · *Import-Export*

Tuesday, 14th October 2003-10-

Dear Lydia and Dr. Romano,

Hope you are both well and fine. You may wonder why I am writing.....but since you are both respected authorities of San Andres, I approach you for subjective support and understanding.

Enclosed herewith is a photocopy of a Courtesy-letter-reply from Prince Charles.....the 5th letter I've received from him after about 15 years of "Growing-up" into the western ways of mentality-attitudes and inculturation. I am and had been working towards a World Peace Project, the fulfilment of the Prophecy of Our Lady of Fatima for World Peace which is anchored subjectively in the Vatican through His Holiness Pope John Paul 11 and objectively through Prince Charles. I'd been receiving Courtesy-acknowledgement-letters from the Pope since 1981.

I need your subjective support on this behalf- just a little kind thought and understanding and a little prayer occasionally for the forward growth of this Prphecy of Our Lady of Fatima for World Peace which I am executing. I, too, want to write about Nanay and her unfinished house in the corner of Divino Rostro. That disturbs my peace of mind. That could have been done already in the past were it not for Nanay's stubborn ways of doing things and her attitudes. While Geny was still in Australia, he wanted to help but Nanay wanted to do it her style- "padi-it-di-it" under her supervision. Also, a few years ago, Telly and Baby Dalisay would have had that done in the proper way, by having an architect-contractor-builder but when Sol found it out, he told Baby and Telly that he would handle the responsibility of building it. I don't know what Sol and Nanay agreed to do but the construction stopped and I never even received any letter about it. And I don't know what happened to the money that was allocated towards building even a small bungalow only, but resistant to typhoons. Nano, too, wanted to have a small and little house-hut in his lot for Nanay where she can store her "very old and tatty books, newspapers and other junks" but Nany did not want them moved from that house in the corner. It is Nanay- her thinking is of the old way.....she does not understand the present day world's objective style of living.....she is set in her old ways.....in fact, Tatay and I used to discuss her subjective ways of thinking through letters when he was still alive. Tatay had been very good to me- we were very, very close even if we were separated miles and oceans apart. That bungalow of Tatay's next to Baby Dalisay's bungalow can be redone, repaired and painted and Nanay and Freddy can live there because that house in the corner is really not fit for them to live. But Nanay is so stubborn- she does not understand anything about money at all and she is not used to it, either. Telly sends her some small amount of money every now and then and Telly holds a small bank account of the money I send to her. But at the moment, I don't have money to give away generously. I'm helping my son together with my husband, Alan, who is already retired- in his last year at University and I, too, am studying for a BA/BSc degree in Health and Social Care in the Open University- a distance learning institution and I am also in full-time employment but my salary is just not enough to be generous with money to my family in the Philippines at present. I did not marry a rich man...I did not marry for money...I married for love! So, there's really nothing I can do, right now. I don't intend to visit Calolbon/San Andres for some while or the Philippines. In fact, I don't want to go to Calolbon/San Andres anymore at all. The deaths of both Tatay and Sol are very painful in my heart and mind---those two individuals who were very close to my mind and heart.....!

My letterhead for my World Peace Project is that of my Princess Status. I christened myself so.....I have the right to this, dating back to my ancestors who were royals in Nanay's part of the family. Tia Betty, Nanay's youngest sister who died in 1986, told me about the royalness of their ancestors and I have grasped that right to be royal...I had anyway been always a Role Model ever since I was born...and I need this royal status for executing this fulfilment of the Prophecy of Our Lady of Fatima for World Peace. Anyway, this would be an honour, too, in the future for our country and for our beloved little town of Calolbon/San Andres. I've already had two letters from Pres. Cory Aquino and one from Pres. Fidel Ramos in their time of office.

So, please support me in this project towards World Peace by thinking kind thoughts of me occasionally and saying a little prayer now and then for me. I would be grateful if you'd just be patient and understanding to my Nanay for after all,, our family had been Role Models in the past and I know that Nanay's contemporaries and friends in the distant past who are now living well-off in America had been inspired by our past family status. And Nanay too, had done quite a bit for the ordinary people of Calolbon such as those cottage industry that she had had for the Calolbon people in the past.

My ancestral heritage-link dated back to the Divine Rights of Kings and Emperors- I found this out in one of my trances in December 1992 when I got fragmented, when I thought I would have died but the Vatican sustained me and for eleven years, I was silent and had, had to sort myself out and grow up in the objective sense of the world...-a very, very expensive "growing-up" physically, emotionally, mentally, spiritually and even monetarily !!!The last aspect was a growing-down instead of growing up.

Thank you ever so much. My kind regards and best wishes to you both.

Yours sincerely,

Urding

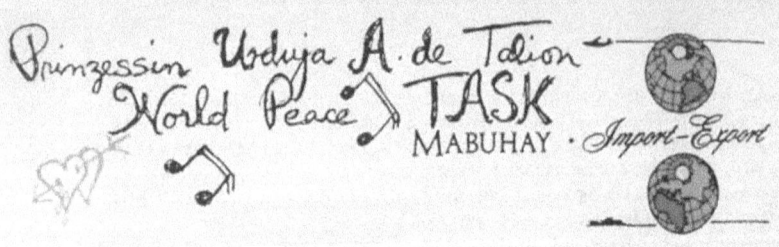

Christine Allen,
CIIR Executive Director,
Unit 3, Canonbury Yard,
190 A New North Road,
Islington, London N1 7BJ

Dear Christine,

May I call you Christine and do away with formality. Thank you.

Thank you for sending me the first issue of Interact; despite the fact that I have ignored virtually all of the correspondences that came from CIIR for several years now. I had been slowly and gradually sorting out not only my personal and private life but also my World Peace Project..... Hope you'll forgive me.

Yes, I have my own individual World Peace Project which I have started so long ago, in fact, I do believe that it had been predestined for me ever since I was born ! I am sustained by the Vatican in the subjective aspect of my project. In fact, I have written about this to Mari King years ago and I have sent her copies of my letters to the Pope, to Prince Charles, maybe even to The Queen and so on.

Herewith is a copy of my recent letter to Prince Charles and a photocopy of his Courtesy-reply from his secretary. This is the 5th letter that I've received from him since many years ago. This short reply from the Prince has motivated me to start all over again with my World Peace project. And because your Interact document arrived together with the enclosed letter from the Prince, last Monday, I've concluded that this was an act of the Holy Spirit showing me the pathway to tread with this project…..hence, this correspondence; and I'd been thinking that your goodselves would be my channels of support through the grace of God…..that I must establish a partnership with you on behalf of this World Peace project…..this time it would have to be the Objective aspect of my project that I must execute, and that I must start being a proper member of CIIR again.

Subjective Aspect of my Task/Project – EX CATHEDRA Doctrine of the One Supreme Bearer which had been blessed and acknowledged by His Holiness Pope John Paul 11, informally, way back in the early 1980's. as well as by Her Royal Majesty, The Queen and of Course, Prince Charles.
Objective Aspects- Mentalities, Attitudes and Mental Health- which is also about "changing and maintaining Minds, understanding Hearts, amalgamation and co-ordination of Minds, Hearts and Bodies, not changing but maintaining Lives….."

Subjective Support needed: occasional kind thoughts and prayers on behalf of the outward, objective growth of this Task/Project
Objective Support needed: to use some of your tangible resources such as publication media, conferences, etc. for the continued growth and development and activisation of my project for World Peace.

To be direct but hopefully, I'm not being rude…if I am, please do forgive me- I need your publication media and some help from your Editor or some qualified writers for advice. At present, I have a book of Poems needing to be published (printout copies which I sent to Prince Charles) into a book and my autobiographical novel which I need to finish typing, and publication of this book will action the objective aspects of my World Peace project, hoping too, that some of the monetary benefits will help me pay up some of my debts and loans which I used for my growing-up and for my self-development so I would be able to Objectivise the Subjectivisation of my task/project…..also to help finance my World Peace project. And of course, I would donate money to CIIR's projects out of the profits realised from my books and future ones as time goes by. What are your rules and conditions for this matter? Please let me know. I thank you in advance.

I enclose a cheque for £26 = 95 (£6 – 95 for the book, Regaining Lands and £20 – 00 for my membership fee.

My gratitude, kind regards and best wishes and I hope you will stand by me in my project for World Peace.

Yours sincerely,

Mrs. Antonia Urduja Talion Roberts

United Nations Association
of Great Britain and Northern Ireland

3 Whitehall Court - London SW1A 2EL
Telephone: 020 7930 2931
Fax: 020 7930 5893
E-mail: info@una-uk.org Website: www.una-uk.org

A Company Limited by Guarantee Registered in England no 2885557 Registered Office 3 Whitehall Court SW1A 2EL

Mrs A Roberts

9 February 2004

Dear Mrs Roberts

Thank you for your recent enquiry regarding membership to the United Nations Association. I am delighted to enclose information about our work, a membership application form and a copy of our latest membership magazine.

The UNA is an organisation that works in the UK to educate, fundraise and campaign to help turn the ideals of the UN into a reality. Although we are independent of the UN itself we often work with, and for, the UN and its agencies. In fact we are the only group in the UK who are committed to working for a world where the UN is the central agency for creating a more peaceful, just and sustainable world.

A standard membership is £25 a year with reductions for those under 26 or on a low income. For this you will receive our new members pack, our quarterly magazine and the opportunity to join our urgent action network and receive more briefings on UNA campaigns.

In addition to the many important tasks carried out by UNA from its headquarters in Whitehall Court, there is an active Branch structure throughout the country. Over 100 Branches provide an opportunity for our members to work together to achieve the aims of the UNA within their local communities.

I hope you find the enclosed interesting and if you have any further queries regarding membership of UNA please do not hesitate to contact me.

Yours in Peace,

Ed Brenton
Membership services officer

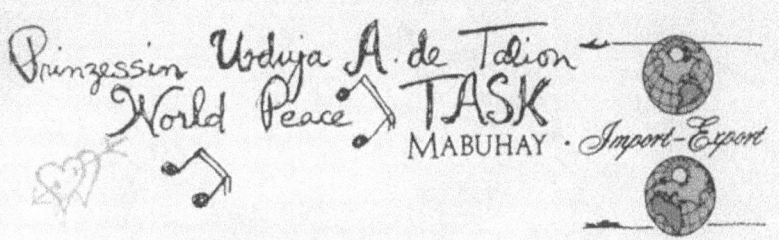

12 February 2004-02-13
Ed Brenton,
United Nations Association-UK
3 Whitehall Court,
London SW1A 2EL

Dear Mr. Brenton,

Thank you for your letter dated 9 February 2004 and enclosures. I enclose herewith Sponsor-membership fee and a few details about myself and of what I am doing.

I obtained information about your goodselves through the invitation to join the 8th Annual Lobby of Parliament in the House of Commons on the 16th March 2004, which the Catholic Institute for International Relations enclosed with their correspondence sent to me. I'd been a member of CIIR circa around 1993 and I have attended a few of their conferences, seminars and meetings around London. I have not been an active member, yet they keep me up-to-date with infos on their activities and programmes.

I am doing a Research on Mental Health- Mentalities, Attitudes, Feelings, Emotions and Nerves... Diversified Nerves which is one of the major factors related to Stress causing Misunderstanding that is a major hindrance to PEACE...!

Thank you once more and my kind regards,

Yours sincerely,

Mrs. Antonia Urduja Talion Roberts

Creative Authors Ltd.
11 A Woodlawn Street,
Whitstable, Kent
CT5 1HQ

Director: Isabel Atherton

Dear Ms Isabel Atherton,

I read your name and business details from the Writers' & Artists' Yearbook 2012. And I thought, perhaps, that my book would fit the type of subject matters that you are dealing with as a literary agent.

I've decided to take the opportunity to send you the full manuscript of my book entitled: Lucifer's Fantasy-Dream. Word count of about 50,000. Although it is supposed to be fiction, yet it deals with the Ex Cathedra doctrine of the church and my prayers attached thereto have been acknowledged and blessed unofficially by His Holiness Pope John Paul 11, as well as the present Pope, Her Royal Majesty, The Queen, Prince Charles and many others.

For some credentials, I enclose the synopsis of my book, letters from some important personages that I've written to while writing this novel for inspiration and human strength, an old CV, a letter from Harper and Row in London, but I'd been sending writing materials from Harper and Row in New York years ago in the eighties and they have always replied to me with short, inspirational replies. My enclosed first book which is autobiographical was self-published. I was very pleased at the start of the publication but I've eventually decided not to sell this book anymore.

I've already got my third book in my head and in my scribbles and notes. It is something which is relevant somehow, in one way or another, to Lucifer's Fantasy-Dream, but it is also relevant to Caring. I'm working part-time as a night care assistant in a small residential home and I'd been working as a Carer since 1994 in various shifts. Caring for old people is a very timely subject matter as it is such a controversial issue which is gaining attention in the media and various departments in the government.

Yours sincerely,

Mrs. Antonia Urduja Talion Roberts

16 August 2012

President: David Kent,
Harper Collins Publishers Ltd.,
2 Bloor Street East,
20th Floor, Toronto,
Ontario, Canada
M4W 1A8

Dear Mr. Kent,

    I have great interest and respect in your publications because I used to send articles and poems to Harper & Row, New York, way back in the 1980s and the 1990s. Harper and Row always sent me acknowledgements and sometimes, inspiring comments.

I enclose herewith my manuscript for my second book which is very relevant to my Issues on World Peace, specialising in Mental Health. The EX CATHEDRA Doctrine which only a Pope can officially proclaim Infallible appeared to me in cloud forms in a transubstantiationary-vision way back in November/December 1972, while I was on evening duty as a front office cashier in the then Skyline Hotel near Heathrow Airport, which is now the Sheraton Skyline Hotel. My Ex Cathedra prayer at the end of the novel was unofficially acknowledged and blessed by His Holiness Pope John 11 and Her Royal Majesty Queen Elizabeth 11.

This spiritual novel can be both for children and adults. Most of all, publication of this book will lead me onwards to my Task for World Peace specialising in Mental Health which I will hold you in gratitude forever. Although this is fiction, there is truth in it and publication of this book is a channel for Peace through the issues on Mental Health which I am able to share and build upon. In this novel, I want to humanise the divine for clearer understanding.

Maybe you might think that it needs updating. If that is so, I am ready to write the updates with Issues you might think worthwhile. Thank you very much for reading this letter of mine and I pray you'll proceed to read the other enclosures as well as the novel.

Yours sincerely,

Mrs. Antonia U. Roberts

The Echo

My issue this time is my EX CATHEDRA DOCTRINE of the ONE SUPREME BEARER- in Whom Everything is contained and Who sustains Everything, the Mightiest and the most Supreme of Them and of Us All, Who has both Divine Nature and Human Nature, Whose Divine Nature and Divine Love borne Almighty God the Father, our Creator, God the Son, our Redeemer Jesus Christ, God the Holy Spirit, our Sanctificator; Whose Human Nature and Human Love borne the Human Mischief, the Reconciled Angel Lucifer, the Bearer of Light, All united in Oneness with One Another, in Union with the Church Triumphant, the Church Militant and the Church Sufferings- All working together for the Oneness of Divine Nature and Human Nature, for the coming of God's Kingdom into the World, for the Peaceful Destiny of Humanity and for the solution to the Mystery of Life Everlasting. Amen.

Although, I'd been writing to the Holy Father since 1970 on various matters, the first acknowledgement I received came from Pope John Paul 11, in 1984, whofrom I'd received about 10 letters. And, this EX CATHEDRA Doctrine was a Transubstantiationary-Vision to me in Cloud Forms way back in November/December 1972 while I was on late duty shift in the then Skyline Hotel, now Sheraton Skyline Hotel near Heathrow airport, as a Front Office Cashier. The Spiritual Forces and the Joy and Happiness that permeated and pierced my Mind, Heart and Nervous System were enormous and powerfully strong. The Message was totally beyond the grasp of Human comprehension then, that I merited not an OBE or an MBE but a one month confinement in the moonlight unit and 10 ECTs (?) in the West Middlesex Hospital

The Essence of this EX CATHEDRA Message was acknowledged and blessed unofficially by Queen Elizabeth 11, Pope John Paul 11, Prince Charles, King Hussein of Jordan, President Ronald Reagan (RIP), the then Presidents Cory Aquino and Fidel Ramos of the Philippines, , Mr. John Major, Mr. Tony Blair and many other important personages around the world.

Spiritualism describes this as a Psychic Experience. It studies and researches into similar Phenomena ; Stanstead Hall, Essex being the main centre for these researches. This Doctrine is relevant to Mental Health, thus my Objective researches on phenomena relevant thereto..

Thine in the One Supreme Bearer, Princess Urduja A. de Talion
Das Humourvolle Spatzlein, Urda von Deutschland
Yours humbly, Mrs. Antonia U. Roberts of the U.K.

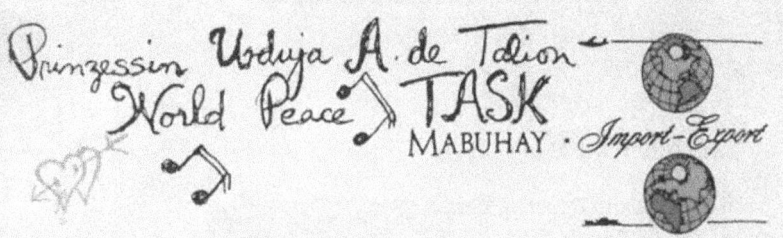

Liebe Helga, Liebe Hilde, Liebe Agnes,

    Hoffentlich seid Euch Alle gut und gesund.

Ich werde Munchen wieder besuchen am 21sten Juni, Freitag bis Montag, 24 sten Juni 2013. Und bleibe wieder in HEH (Hotel Europaischer Hof)

Habt Euch LUST nach Salzburg zu fahren und Spazieren zu gehen am Samstag, 22sten Juni ? Ich werde im Dom zu besuchen und zu beten. Irgendwann im Jahre 1996 (?) hatte ich eine Apparition von Heilige Mutter Gottes Maria von Alttoting im Dom im Salzburg gehabt. Ich wurde umgesund, damals- post natal depression.

Meine jungste Schwester, Telly, besuche uns und bleibe mit uns am 2sten Mai bis 18sten Juni 2013. Wir werden uns viel verreisen hier im UK. Sollte Telly Visa nach Frankreich bekamme, dann wurden meine Tochter, Elsie, Telly und Ich nach Paris zu fahren mit dem Eurostar von 7ten bis 10ten Juni., Freitag bis Montag. Am 11ten Juni, fliegt Elsie nach die Turkei um Triathlon, Gross Britannia zu representieren und fliegt zuruck nach England am 16sten Juni. Und dann, fliege ich nach Munchen am 21sten bis 24sten Juni 2013.

Ich werde mich sehr, sehr Glucklich meine Lieben Damen- Helga, Hilde und Agnes, wieder zu sehen und im Salzburg Spazieren zu gehen. Wir konnen im meinem hotel treffen und dann fahren wir mit dem Zug aus Hauptbahnhof. Was sagen Sie daran?

Viele Lieben Grussen.

Urduja

Ang Bituin Ng Aking Buhay

Ikaw ay isang Bituin ng Langit,
At ako naman ay isang Buwan....
Ang Nanay nang lahat
Na mga Bituin !
Ang Araw ay nagbibigay ng
Illuminacion para sa iyo at
Para sa lahat na mga
Bituin sa Langit.
Ang Araw din, ay nag illuminar sa
Buwan at ang Buwan ay
Nag bibigay ng Liwanag sa
Mundo, sa Universo, sa
Constellacion at sa lahat
Na mga bagay-bagay kung gabi.
Ako-and Buwan- ay umiibig !
Iniibig ko and aking Pamilya,
Iniibig ko ang Natur
Iniibg ko ang mga Angeles sa Langit
Iniibig ko ang lahat na Bagay...
At iniibig ko ang Diyos,
Ang Creador ng Langit at Mundo
At mga Tao!
Sapagkat kung wala ng Diyos,
Ay hindi tayo mabubuhay !

The Star Of My Life

You are a Star in the Firmament,
And, I am the Moon..
The Mother of all the Stars!
The Sun gives Illumination to the Moon
And the Moon gives Light to
The World, the Universe, the Constellation
And to Everything, at Night.
I -the Moon - give Love!
I love my Family,
I love Nature,
I love all the Angels in Heaven,
I love everything...
And, I love God, the Creator of the Heavens
And of Everything in it
Because without God, all of us won't exist and live.

Die Sternen Meines Lebens

Du bist eine Sterne auf den Firmamenten,
Ich bin der Mond....die Mutter von allen Sternen!
Die Sonne erleuchtet fur Dich und fur allen Sternen auf den Himmel -
Die Sonne auch erleuchtet die Erde, den Universe,
das Constellazion und allen Sachen, in die Nacht;
Ich-der Mond- liebe!
Ich liebe meine Familie,
Ich liebe die Natur,
Ich liebe die Engels auf den Himmel
Und ich liebe allen Sachen...
Ich liebe den Gott,
Schopfer des Himmels
Und die Erden;
Ohne Gott, allen Sachen und
Wir alles uberall koennen
Nichts existieren und leben.

La Estrella De Mi Vida

Tu estas una Estrella en la Firmamente,
Y yo estoy la Luna.... la
Madre de todos Estrellas!
El Sol dar la Illuminacion para ti
Y para todos Estrellas en los Cielos.
El Sol, tambien illuminar la Luna y
La Luna illuminar la Tierra,
El Universo, la Constellacion
Y todas Cosas por las Noches.
Yo- la Luna- amo!
Yo amo mi Familia y amo
Natur, Yo amo los Angeles
En los Cielos y Yo amo todas Cosas...
Y yo amo el Dios, el
Creador de los Cielos y
De la Tierra.
Sin el Dios, todas Cosas y nosotros
No pueden Exister!

Echoes of My Mind

Chapter III

These magical-rendezvous with Love-poems were written when I was pregnant with my first child in 1976. At that time, I was also working as a Bookkeeper/Accountant in an Import-Export Jewish Family Firm. The circumstances surrounding my pregnancy were very stressful- neurologically stressful, what with parties here and there and weekend home-visits with my Filipina friends married to Englishmen and their having babies, too...

I begot post-natal depression, the medical term being 'puerperal psychosis.' While in Labour, I was praying the Holy Rosary, putting on make-up on my face- lipstick, blush-on, eye-liner, eyebrow pencil, reading and writing poems I!! Baby refused to come out and I was finally given a Caesarian Operation, after twenty-seven hours of hard-labour, which I believed that without this last recourse, I would have died.

Love, Faith, Hope and Prayers carried me through.

Thanks the good Lord for that...

Antonia Urduja Roberts

Chapter III

Echoes Of My Mind
Chapter III-: Twenty-four sets of my Poems written during the Seventies.

1) My Dream Vision
2) The Journey Of Life
3) The Jolly Damsel
4) The Treasures Of Life
5) The Starlight Of The Night
6) The Dawn Of Glory
7) Beautiful Summer
8) The Awakening
9) Joyful Happiness
10) The Melody Of Music
11) The Joyful Splendor Of Love
12) The Conquering Love
13) The Brilliance Of Love
14) Nostalgia
15) The Ballad Of East and West by Rudyard Kippling and My Version Of It
16) The River Of Life
17) Dawn Of Humanity
18) Argue About Shadows
19) The Meadows By The Seashore
20) Undaunted Radiance
21) The Nectar Of Life
22) The Sunshine Of Life
23) Predestined Loveliness
24) My Way To Jerusalem.

My Dream Vision

I must jubilantly rejoice
To the sound of the angel's voice,
Their melodious tune is what I seek
And their character which is meek.

I see heavenward the vast kingdom
Whose inhabitants are full of wisdom,
They are full of love and affection
And they sing in joyful exaltation.

As I climb the hill, I see the gate
To the heavenly abode which is a state
Of glorious and radiant happiness
Which is never impaired by sadness.

Then I awake from my dream
And I go to the nearby stream,
To bathe myself with the coolness of the water
Because I am a soul in a living matter.

The Journey Of Life

Life is full of glorious dream,
Pouring out like a milky cream,
It is filled with love and inspiration
Ending to a series of imagination.
But the more we fail
The more we must travail
To reap the fruits of success
And forget our further stress.

Life sails on like a ship at sea
Through stormy ways it makes a plea,
It flies like the airplanes in the sky
Passing every wandering cloud trailing by.
Life rejuvenates like the trees in spring
Harbouring birds that gleefully sing
Melodious tunes in the air
Which in winter is very rare.

Life is like a battlefield
Full of soldiers not willing to yield
In the fight against the enemies
Committing several calumnies.
Life goes on and soon it's over,
As death lifts up our books' cover,
Brave and heroic deeds are rewarded
To our heavenly abode which never gets crowded.

The Jolly Damsel

She awakes from her dream
And goes to the nearby stream,
The pearls of the morning dew
To her is an experience new.

She wades in the water pool
And feels it is extremely cool,
She washes her pinky cheek
And her body that is satin-sleek.

On her hair alights a butterfly
"How I wish, like you, I can fly!
On my hair have a rest
So to fly again, you will have zest."

The butterfly whispers in her ear
As she feels very eager to hear,
"I'll give you a golden chord
That will give your life joyful accord."

She fondles the chord with utmost dalliance
As slowly in her mind occurs the brilliance
Of love and generosity to the poor,
Who can lead one to the heavenly door.

The Treasures of Life

When in our garden I repose
I see a steadily blooming rose,
Then on my head alights a lark
Which leaves in my intuition a mark.

The water in the pool is crystal clear
So I take off the clothes I wear,
The coolness gives me pleasure
And its nearness is a treasure.

At a distance stands a rock
To see it moves, gives me a shock,
When I go near it, it gives me wisdom
Because it forms a tiny kingdom.

Beneath the rock is an anthill
Its inhabitants are never still,
In the nearby tree is a beehive
With a queen bee keeping her subjects alive.

The crows fly and occasionally swerve
Sometimes they get on my nerve,
But their presence enables me to write a story
So if they fly to and fro, I never worry.

My most precious treasure is my husband
He is like the fairies' magic wand,
Words of love and wisdom to me he sprinkles
Like a star in the sky, he often twinkles.

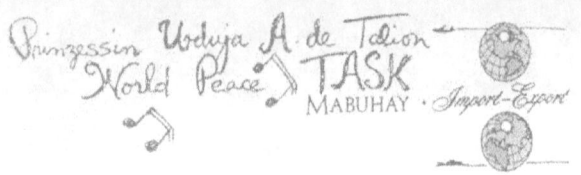

The Starlight Of The Night

Ignorance causes intellectual darkness
Illumined by a starlight into brightness,
The Lord's glorious resurrection
For a joyful life is a foundation.

Our spiritual progress is measured by God's promises
So that we may enter the heavenly premises,
The will of the Lord we must follow
Whether ours is shallow or hollow.

Dream about the brightness of the night
Whereby angels dance in wonderlight,
My soul's horizon is higher than the highest peak
And cherubims discover that my nature is not weak.

Flowers are a joy for those who labour
And fill their hearts with glorious splendour,
Light illumines night and glorifies day
And paves a bright prospect to those who labour in every way.

The Dawn of Glory

Has he ever been so keen
The wonders of dawn to have seen,
The dewdrops cling to the plants
Telling Him, the Master Sun, of their wants.

The swift breeze of dawn he feels
As the gardener pulls the wheels
Of the cart with the newly-cut branches
And flowers clustered in bunches.

The Daystar slowly arises
As He brings pleasant surprises
To the trees, buds and flowers
Hiding in their aromatic bowers.

As the river's water warp
The bee's stings become sharp,
That is the wisdom of man's folly,
Which in this world makes us jolly.

Beautiful Summer

The day is glorified by the sunbeam
The night is illumined by the moonbeam,
The waters flawlessly flow from the fountains
And from waterfalls originating from the mountains.

Day and night the sun and moon sway
Sharing happiness with us in every way,
The hills are grazed by flocks of sheep
They eat, drink, run and sleep.

Now the sea is governed by the summer-tide
It extends over the ocean, which is very wide,
With frothy waves it does appear
It never stops throughout the year.

Dozens of eggs the hens lay
Amidst their nests made of hay,
When the day is gay, hens, roosters and chicks dance around
With utmost happiness among them that abound.

Ducks, geese and swans on the pond swim
While swimming, they look very prim,
When I develop my gift, them I will command
To get out from the water and walk on the land.

Several children mould pots of clay
With them they build a house and play,
Like a family living with zest
Who's always on the go and never stops to rest.

The Awakening

You are the God of the early mornings
You are the God of the late evenings,
And when your followers perish in the fight
You come to me very, very late at night.

My spirit undergoes a white funeral
Which for the body is supernatural,
I look above and envision You in my dreams
I even see You amidst the flowing streams.

Amidst the height of the mountain peak
Explores my spirit which is not weak,
The depth of Your thoughts I cannot reach
Please send me the Holy Spirit, my soul to teach.

When Your heavenly motives I cannot trace
Because they pertain to the whole race,
Yet, to my utmost I must labour
And must implant in my heart the deepest fervour.

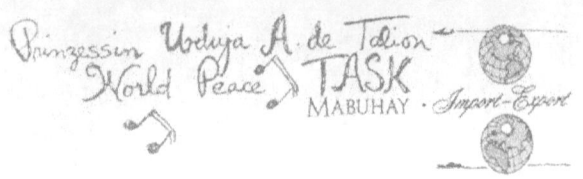

Joyful Happiness

Happiness is music in the air
And it is beauty of a life began,
It vibrates through this glorious fair
Like the aura of the rising sun.

Happiness is a robin flying gleefully
And singing a melodic harmony,
It is a waterfall cascading endlessly
Emanating a rhythmical symphony.

Happiness is the continual ticking of a clock
Reminding us to do good work everyday,
It is the endless crowing of a cock
Expressing contentment in every way.

The Melody Of Music

The lilting sound of delightful music
Is valued as supremely intrinsic,
It gives us spiritual elevation
And teaches children cultural education.

It abounds a concert hall with symphony
As the audience applauds in harmony,
It lulls a crying infant to sleep
And makes a lonely adult pathetically weep.

Springtime music is in the air
Sung by the birds whose colours are fair,
Music emanates as the wind blows
As the cock crows and the river flows.

The inspirational choir music creates jubilation
Which to the Almighty God we offer exaltation,
Because its beauty originates from Him
In this bright world, which is spiritually, dim.

The Joyful Splendour Of Love

My love for Him was full of glory
Which sprung out from my childhood,
From the time grandma told me the story
Of His joyful and happy infanthood.

His mother Mary gave Him full of affection
Its beauty in our minds we must ponder,
Every day and every night I was full of recollection
Of His glorious life full of wonder.

Now I fell in love with a respectable man
Who amidst the park of love I had seen,
He was lovable, understanding and a gentleman
Full of sadism he had never been.

We offered our love to the glory of the Lord
Who shone like the sun in this life,
He was the world's promised Word
And we had to adore Him, as man and wife.

The Conquering Love

Amidst the lustrous wonders of the universe
You sought for me while I slept
With my eyes closed and bereft
Of my heart, surrounded by people who wept;
Because the bridge of love they could not traverse.

Yes, I once felt the bliss of ignorance
Of not loving You because my heart was wrapped up in material prosperity,
Then You begged me for charity...
"Of what?" I asked, "Faith, Hope and Charity to give you life's longevity,"
I looked at You and prayed, You are my life's felicity,
Myself I completely surrender to You, and I went into trance.

I sought for You amidst the birds, the trees and the flowers
And found the embers of your undying love for humanity
That could give the world peace and tranquility
That I could lead everyone to that Utopic certainty-
Are secretly hidden in their aromatic bowers.

The Brilliance Of Love

The stars appear luminous
As if the signs are ominous
Of the last judgment day
When angels in the heaven sway.

Within our world's generation
There will occur a regeneration
When the love of the Lord shines in the dark
And everyone will exclaim, "Hark the lark!"

Joy and exaltation will prevail
The spiritual labourers will travail
Until they reach their destination
Which is the Supreme One's predestination.

The pure love in our hearts is our salvation
And the Lord will give us His sanctification,
As we rejoice in joyful exaltation
As a fruit of His sorrowful redemption.

Of Gods existence we must be certain
But in all our ways we have to be uncertain,
That is the brilliance of the love
Of the Supreme Lord from above.

Nostalgia

Within the shadow
Of doubt and uncertainty,
I then walk by the sea
To watch the beauty
At the end of the day.
Sunset enhances the atmosphere
And illuminates the vast horizon
With a prismatic display of colours.
My thoughts meander to my youth-
Vibrant, carefree and gay
As the lilies of the valley;
Pliable, soft and silky
Like the waves of the sea;
But unenlightened about
The grandeur of the day.
Then I contemplate about
My life as of today-
Vibrant, but careful, still gay
And semi-enlightened about
The splendour of the day.

Slowly darkness envelops the atmosphere,
As the Daystar descends from
His resplendent throne;
His heavenly shades, begin to fade
And His golden sheen is nowhere to be seen.
The leaves of the trees
Showered by His tender caress
Do bid adieu to His embraces.
A gigantic darkness prevails,
Sunless...moonless.... starless...
Unilluminated
Except by man-made inventions,
Nevertheless beauteous, though not splendorous.
I then find myself in introspection,
Speculating about sleep-
A relief from tedium and a replica of death!

I gaze back toward the heavens,
And conceive the ever-brilliant Sun

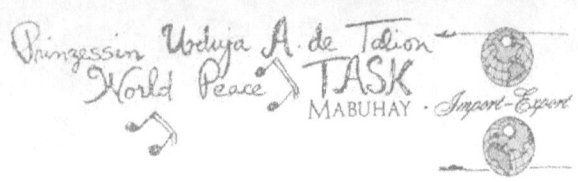

Shining behind the clouds.
My thoughts meander again
To a new tomorrow-
Sunrise after the night!
Vibrant, cheerful and full of Sunshine,
A resplendent lustre of hope.

The Ballad Of East And West- Rudyard Kipling (1865-1956)

Oh, East is East, and West is West,
And never the Twain shall meet,
Till Earth and Sky stand presently
At God's Great Judgment Seat;
But there is neither East nor West,
Border nor Breed, nor Birth,
When two strong men stand face to face,
Though they come from the Ends of the
Earth!

My Version of the Above:

Oh East needs West, and West needs East
And gradually the Twain shall meet,
When the Strong-Weakness of a man
And the Weak-Strength of a woman,
Defy the Earth and Sky standing at
God's great Judgment Seat;
And the thunderous Silence within the
Heart beckons Lightning and Thunder,
Hurricane and Storm and the Ends of the Earth,
To bridge the Gaps imposed by Border and Breed,
And Birth, by East and West
And the Silent Thunder of the Mind ordains the Destiny for -
PEACE!

By Princess Urduja A. De Talion - Antonia

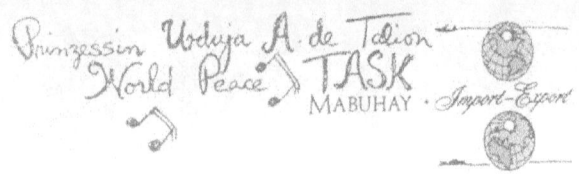

The River Of Life

The water floweth through the river of life
Which is a struggle against suffering
That should, to the Lord, be made an offering,
Because the struggle against it causes more suffering
And redemptive tears of love that floweth through the river of life.

The passion of Jesus is the redemptive love
Which is capable of raising up the world
Because the supernatural graces, it offers, are manifold
So to develop genuine love in our hearts we must be bold
To awaken the sleeping humanity through Jesus' redemptive love.

The river of life imparts joy,
Which is the calm and interior serenity
Profound peace and life's longevity
Abdication of oneself to the Lord in totality-
So that through one's veins will flow the blood that imparts joy.

In this river, man can grow through sufferings,
If instead of resigning himself to them
He struggles against them
And into his upward climb integrates them,
In this way man develops his faculties and grow through sufferings.

Dawn Of Humanity

As the stars fade one by one from the sky
The garment of darkness is shed at the end of the night
As the sun starts to shine its early light
And the plant and animal kingdom explain with all their might
'The dawn of humanity, we readeth in the sky!'

We must fight for the preservation of beauty,
Beauty of wisdom and of the intellect,
If all the vicissitudes of life we must recollect
Those that beareth good fruits we must select
To fight for the preservation of beauty.

The world is a sepulcher of great men
Who are lovers of beauty and wisdom,
Who keep their intellect busy to relieve their feelings of boredom
So that they can give account in the heavenly kingdom
They that fill the world with beauty and wisdom are great men.

As earthly kings and queens are crowned
We will hear the sweet call of the blue sea-bird of spring;
Joy, love and happiness to our spirits it will bring
Because the wisdom in the sky it will sing
As the dawn approaches when the one complete emperor will be crowned.

Argue About Shadows

My goddess rises from the dead with life in each hand
As I rise early with the Sun and commune with nature,
The shadows they cast harmoniously my spirit nurture
And enable me to design the heavenly structure
As my spirit rises with every world event with life in each hand.

I build a wall of thought in which evil intentions shoots off like arrows,
While the sands over the silent desert cultivate my mind,
As supernatural desires with my spirit they bind
So that the foundations of life's shadows I can find,
While my mind the world's evil shoots off like arrows.

The brightness of the one that loveth
Is a short beam of struggling light that casts shadows
While we, the beholders, we must open our spirits' windows,
So that our hungering hearts can enjoy love's meadows
As love illuminates in the eyes of the one that loveth.

Into the pure waters of love, we must the spirit of hatred not poureth,
We must follow the God's principles of love
And drink the waters of love to enable our spirits to rise above
So that they can be illuminated by the heavenly love
If we, into the world, the spirit of hatred not poureth.

The Meadows By The Seashore

Behold the flowers are utmostly sweeter
Than the bees flying to Peter-
The gardener in these vibrant meadows
Which in the afternoons are full of shadows
Cast by the spell of the setting Sun.
Peter fills a grand tun
With pure, cool water and wine-
And to the plants he will scatter
Every drop..
Then the butterfly, the plant reaches
For his rival bees he watches
So they won't come near the flowers-
And his compliment to her he can shower
When the pollens are dropped into the grounds.
The butterfly does several rounds
Beneath the flowers. And picks aglow
Several pollens in the air that blow-
The bees gallantly prattle
And they begin to startle
The sleeping hibiscus and roses
While the butterfly on the plant reposes.
Then the bees alight on the turf
While the whispering surf
Dashes vivaciously ashore
Not far from Peter who does the chore.
To one another, they then speak
With a language not of the weak
But of the brave young lad
Who does the world's newest fad.

Undaunted Radiance

The Lord's second incarnation
Will bring forth great jubilation,
The angels will dance by wonderlight
And the people will rejoice by starlight.

Our spirits need spiritual elevation
And we have to eschew every evil temptation,
To the Lord we must give our utmost worship
To create with Him a radiant love-relationship.

Our own free will within us reside
Although to God's will we must abide,
We should forget our earthly vanity
And cultivate fervour and thought purity.

Our earthly pleasure to Him we must relinquish
We must do this without signs of anguish,
Past and future things are of deep immensities
To stand apart and look into them are Life's necessities.

Knowing the radiant truth makes our souls ecstatic
And enables the body to feel fantastic;
His radiance from above will bring forth bliss
The church triumphant and militant one another will kiss.

The Nectar Of Life

Drink deep the nectar of life, my friend
Drink it with appreciation and in no mad haste
So that the wisdom of folly will not go to waste
As this is blessed wisdom the uplifted man can taste
Let your veins abound with the nectar of life, my friend.

The man who harvests the fruit of experience
Will inwardly feel the joy of the spirit
His constant struggles will abound in merit
And he will eternally progress in body and in spirit
And will be conscious of the wisdom of the fruits of experience.

Heaven on earth exists not far
Pure love in our hearts will be cultivated
The guilt of evil deeds will be eradicated
Part of divinity with our humanity will be transubstantiated
Then we will see that heaven on earth exists not far.

Sorrow and bereavement are the clouds that come along with God
As He does not come in clear shining
Sometimes He comes as the flashing lightning
When the love in one's heart is continuously shining
Joy and life everlasting are the offshoots of the clouds that
come along with God.

The Sunshine Of Life

Behold the glimmering starlight
Vanishing from our sight,
Humanity must abound in servitude
To the Lord in greater magnitude.

When all the suffering and pain
The body can attain,
The soul will experience bliss
And He will give him a benevolent kiss.

Joy is the wonderlight
Vibrating through this earthly night,
Rapture and delight it will bring
Which will enable the angels to sing.

Let us jubilantly raise
To God songs of praise,
Our love and adoration He searches
And spiritual growth in us He reaches.

As we awake in joyful mood
Looking forward with a good
Foresight towards our spiritual future
The sunshine of our life our souls will enrapture.

Predestined Loveliness

The stars shine with unusual splendour
Which fill me with joyful ardour,
The flames of candles lit in the open air
Impart a twinkling character to my hair.

Is it part of wisdom to persist with kindness
And a part of joy to counteract sadness?
My happiness is as deep as a lagoon
And the kindness in my heart illuminates like the moon.

When the world with His hands He will carry
He must be firm and must never tarry,
He's the Son who will reign as the world's Emperor
And the people will never be filled with terror.

He was a Child of sorrows and will be a Son of joy,
With His feelings, He will never be coy;
People will adore Him, His Will, will be done
And His spirit from His body will never be gone.

My Way To Jerusalem

Our gateway to salvation
Is His sorrowful redemption,
Of man's inhumanity to the Lord
Who comes down as a promised Word.

Jerusalem is our destination
As is written in the Supreme One's predestination,
The lovable longings of our Lord we must satisfy
So our spirits He will sanctify.

The hammerings on to the Cross create extreme pain
That only the Lord Jesus can attain,
His eternal love for us is written in the stars
Which will illumine the world and will pacify wars.

When we seek Jerusalem, sin we must abandon
So the Lord, our mistakes will pardon,
Hymns of love and praise the angels will sing
All for the glory of the Supreme King.

Echoes Of My Mind

Chapter IV

I was an individual person when I met my present husband of forty-one years of marriage. He fell in love with me right away the moment he set eyes on me. In less than a month, we were engaged and we got married in the Registry Office within two months of knowing each other.

Being a successful published writer was a goal and a dream for me to achieve. I conducted a love affair with Writing.... But, I was a made-up individual person, I was set in my ways and it was difficult for me to change my ways!

I took courses with the Open University. Open To Change was my first mini-course. I was, indeed, exuberantly happy and, I made my utmost effort to improve my mentality and incorporate some positive British ways of thinking. I had no money, so I had to work and save some money for my studies.

My children were growing up. I tried to juggle being a Mother to my darling children, a Carer in Care Homes and an OU student. I loved being a Wife and a Mother. I loved being a Carer and I loved being an OU student. My husband loved me and he did his best to help me when I needed him.

My husband worked for BOAC, which amalgamated with BEA and became BA (British Airways.) We travelled a lot with the children...The Philippines, the land of my birth, was a frequent travel destination. How the children enjoyed playing with their cousins! As my husband got further promotions in his job as Engineer with BA, we travelled first-class with British Airways in various parts of the world.

I never finished a degree with the OU, but I graduated from the University of Life with a Doctorate in Humanity. Now, I am gradually and happily writing my way up.

As well as writing, my present project is promoting The Brotherhood of Man and Mental Health to help humanity in small

ways that I could manage within my individual limitations and I am happy in my own little ways....

Antonia Urduja Roberts

Echoes Of My Mind

Chapter IV

Essays and Articles written when I was a student at the Open University, when I was working in various Jobs such as Caring, Bookkeeping and Accounting in an Import-Export Jewish family firm, Front Office Cashier and Night Auditor in two four-star hotels near Heathrow Airport which were skillfully executed with Love and were immensely enjoyable...And, in private moments of Relaxation when my thoughts would skyrocket to the Sun, Moon and Stars in the heavens....

Frolics And Capers In The Office

10 December 1975

Mane. I felt fed up. I wanted to crash and sod everything, soar up to the sky, if possible. I guessed I have worked too hard the previous day. About 11:00 AM, Rita was in the washroom. I went in.

"Rita, I'm in a bad mood. I want to crash and sod everything," I said while clenching my fist.
"Why, has anyone upset you?"
" No, I don't know. I just want to do it."
We both laughed and I went to the loo and had a wee. Afterwards, I went back to my desk to fill in the Purchase Day Book. After about a minute, I couldn't keep still and I still felt fed up. I went down to the warehouse to Wally's office, the manager.
"Wally, Im fed up. I want to crash everything and sod everything. What shall I do?"
Huh?" he answered with his clownish grin and mannerisms. Well, what do you want to do? Break a glass?" He came toward me and saw a plasterboard on the way.
"Here, Tonie, here's something to break. Come on, do it," he said while handing it to me. I put the centre of the board on one of my knees and broke it.
"Ha! Ha! Ha! Do you feel better now? " He asked.
"Not yet! Let's do boxing or karate, " I suggested and we both positioned ourselves as if we were boxing one another jokingly. We both laughed loudly. Later on, I said. "I feel better now."
I then went back upstairs to our office and continued filling in the Purchase Day Book, but yet, I still felt like soaring up to the clouds.
At 11-30 AM, Mr. Freeman went out and promised to be back before 2-OOPM. At about 11-45 AM, I remarked authoritatively.
"Malcolm, I'm going out for my lunch break." Malcolm replied jokingly with a question to David, the boss' son.
"David, Tonie wants to go out. We can't allow her that, can we?" I was furious although I knew that the remark was only a joke. I then said again in an authoritative manner.
"I am entitled for my lunch break!!! And I am going out," there was silence and a pause, then I asked, "Where's the nearest Kentucky Fried Chicken Takeaway from here?"
"The nearest one is in Hounslow West," answered David.

"That's too far. I just want to walk to give me a release. I want to eat something. I haven't eaten for a long time. If I can't have Kentucky Fried Chicken, maybe anchovies and/or cockles will do. Where can I buy cockles?"

"The nearest one is in Brentford High Street. It will take you only about half an hour to walk there, "Malcolm instructed.

"Good, I am going. I'm fed up, you know. I don't know why. I want to crash and sod everything. I am in a very bad mood today!" I explained to them,

"Ohhhhh!!!!" Malcolm uttered.

"What do you think I do feel, Tonie...." David queried.

"I don't know and I don't care. I don't feel what you feel and I don't want to feel what you feel!" I answered David back. There was silence and so I went.

I went to Brentford High Street and bought a roll, anchovies and yoghurt. Then I walked back to the office and ate them there.

David didn't know what to do with me. He felt somewhat uneasy with his dealings toward me and he was very careful not to make any mistake with me.

"I can't always be very good, nice, kind and accommodating all the time, can I? I am only human, so I have to have my outbursts now and then." I lectured David and Malcolm...Malcolm being the right-hand man of the boss.

"Oh yes, in two years time, he will be completely bald and will have to wear a wig!" I countered while gesturing with my forefinger and middle finger into a V, unaware of its rude meaning.

"What did you say, Tonie?" Malcolm queried again.

"Two years," still with my two fingers held up in the form of a v. They laughed and I remembered its rude implication, so I continued- " The trouble with you is that I say and do things innocently and you interpreted them in a rude manner. It's not my fault- it's your fault."

"You know Wally, David's previous girl-friend commented this about him, He's only 23 years old yet he thinks like a 31 year old! "

"Ha! Ha! Ha I and he looks like it, " Malcolm continued and we all laughed. David's humour was cut off and he inwardly became furious. He went to get the small coffee plastic stirrer and threw it to my table.

"That's what you'll get from me!" he exclaimed and we all laughed while David's laughter was very nonchalant "it's all Tonie's fault."

"Of course not, I didn't start it."

" You are the stirrer!"

"No, I'm not. I only supplemented Malcolm's jokes," I mischievously replied with a grin on my face and twinkle in my eyes.

I placed the Purchase' Day Book and other accounts books in the safe and went back to my desk.

"You shouldn't do that to me, Tonie...." David cried with suppressed mixture of feelings and emotions.

" Why not.... You threw it to my desk and I'll threw it to your desk. That's only fair. An eye for an eye, a tooth for a tooth. That's what TALION, my maiden name means. AH.... AH.... So.... So..."

Wally went downstairs back to the warehouse. David and Malcolm continued with some more private conversations, which I was not interested in, so I concentrated on filling the Nominal Ledger Book as I was planning to do a trial balance.

11-40 AM of the 11" December 1975.

Frolics And Capers In The Office

11th December 1975

Mr. Freeman, the boss said, "I don't think I'm going to the bank today. I'll go there tomorrow. Can you think of any reason why I should go, Tonie?"
 "Well there's about £12,500=00 to be deposited...." I replied.
"It's only £12,500=00, that's nothing, isn't it?" Mr. Freeman sounded non-committal.
Malcolm's brows frowned and he remarked. "Well, I wouldn't mind if you'll distribute them between Tonie and me..."
"Ha!!! Ha!! Ha!!!" I laughed. It makes me laugh when I say things like that. Malcolm's face creased again.
"Of course, when you're talking about thousands, it's chicken feed, isn't it? But in our case, my husband and I have to pay our £12,000.00 house for twenty-five years."

11-45 PM on 11th December 1975

David was reading a brochure of Constance-supplies for offices and there was an office desk with a model wearing a long dress.
 "I wonder if they supply these birds as furnishings, as well," David said.
"You bet! You need a girl-Friday cum glamour girl to fill that need in you." I answered.
"What? You can be one", David said.
"No, not me. I'm old already. I've passed already that craving for glamour! " I replied.
"No, you're sexy! " David said.
"Of course, I am, but I'm an old, loving and contented wife with no more need for any eligible man, " I commented.
"How sweet! Say that again..." David joked.
"Of course not, I won't repeat what I've already said. Remember Rita, our typist way back in April 1974'? She was the glamour girl type. She used to come in long dresses and was, indeed, very appealing and sexy..."
"Who? " David asked.
"Rita, of course, you knew her. She told me the time when one of your male friends came to the office. She liked him. He had that book on Bisexuality and Homosexuality, " I said.
" I don't remember!" David exclaimed.

" Of course, you won't. You would not want to remember because you were only a kid then" I said. At the mention of kid, he came near me with a grin and jokingly wanted to strike me with a ruler. I burst into laughter. ! David, Malcolm and I laughed to our hearts' content.
"You stirrer..!"   David pointed at me laughingly and strikes me gently with his ruler.

Excerpts And Snippets On My Self-Psychoanalysis, Self-Healing And Forgiveness
4-20 PM   **Monday**   **27 July 1992**

Why do I have such a big mouth???? . Before I married my husband, I was gentle and discreet and reasonable in my speech. But then, I have gradually developed this 'big mouth, windy speech' and the person who does this is not my normal self. But, I am not a normal person- I guess, that I would have to put up with this other-self, but I must learn to discipline this 'big mouth' and learn from my mistakes because everyone is secretly laughing at me and tactfully refusing my offer of friendship.

Dear Father/Lord God in the One Supreme Bearer and All. Please help me how to put all these behind and use my mistakes last Saturday as a batch of lessons relevant to the objective-public-relationship, with people of various kinds. I have heard them say in different circumstances that they think I feel superior to them. But, in reality, I don't feel superior at all to them. I just feel equality in inequality, maintaining my individual self-respect and not wanting to trample on other peoples' self-respect and pride.

As a newly-arrived parishioner in Frimley, I have felt so much nervous actions and interactions in my local Catholic church. I practice Catholicism as I have learned and imbibed from the country of my birth, the Philippines. We Filipinos are devout Catholics but the practice of my faith and beliefs are interspersed with the religious and superstitious beliefs of our ancestors, as handed down through successive generations. It is a combination of Spanish Catholicism and the pagan-beliefs of our long-bygone ancestors.

It is customary amongst Catholic Filipinos in the olden times, which is still practiced today to consecrate a very sick child/children to either the Blessed Mother, to Jesus or to a particular saint of the parents' choice, in the hope that the child/children would get better. Novenas are encouraged (9-days consecutive prayers, hymns to the saints involved, attendance at Holy Masses, giving alms to the poor, burning candles, kneeling-walking from the main door to the main altar of the church whilst praying the Holy Rosary and other religious practices allied thereto.). But, with the shallowness of the American commercialism and capitalism that deep religious faith

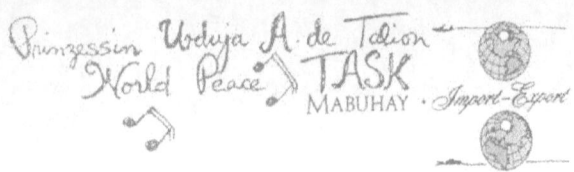

and piety imbibed from the Spanish-Catholic-colonialists have been replaced by yearnings for the fulfillment of their materialistic dreams that the newly-arrived-Americans have introduced in the Philippines.

Before the Spanish-colonialists arrived in the Philippines, there was a communal system of land ownership- land was communally owned. The tillers had full access to and ownership of their produce and the local government officials did not own, but simply administered the communal property in the name of the entire community. But, Spanish colonialism changed this system. The then Spanish Friars and other colonialists who remained in the Philippines and have mostly became the Elites of our country, have petitioned to the then King Philip 11 of Spain for a system of land ownership at their disposal. In fact, as my father, who was a lawyer and a politician when he was still alive joked -Before the Spanish-colonialists arrived in our country, we, the Filipinos had the Land and they had the Bible. We knelt in front of the Spanish-colonialists, they blest us and when we stood up, they had the Land and we had the Bible!'

Religion is a complicated subject matter to discuss. I have viewed interdenominationalism with great strain in my nervous system. I have, however, shared interests in my husband's religion of Spiritualism without relinquishing my Catholic faith.

One of the books on Spiritualism that I've read is about Aura, the atmosphere of a person or place. It has expressed doubt and reservation upon the belief, or is it a fact- that life in the foetus begins at the moment of Conception, at least, that's what we've been taught in our course in Religion in school, college and university. I may even add that the circumstances that brought about the sexual union, which resulted in the fertilization of the egg cell, and the sperm cell would have an effect upon the life-formation of that foetus. In fact, following the logic of the INDENT by Carl Gustav Jung, which is, of course, relevant to the Mendelian Theory of Heredity, the potentials within life formation in the foetus could be traced way, way back from their ancestors far, far removed. That is why, it is, that family solidarity is an important factor in personality development.

Personality development is an important step to growing-up. Aside from the logic of Carl Gustav Jung of the indents and the Mendelian Theory of Heredity and other principles allied thereto, migrations, intermarriages, divorces, human limitations and human imperfections, and other factors could cause personality fragmentation resulting to stress in the nervous system. With personality development, we must take into consideration marriage, although we don't necessarily need to be married to have children. The primary purposes of marriage according to what I've learned from school are, the procreation of children and mutual love and understanding between husband and wife. I certainly don't remember sexual gratification or sexual compatibility as being the third aim because this had been replaced by companionship, although sexual union is an important act in the begetting of children.

Well, that's the way life is. We are Equal only because we are not Equal- we are Equal in our Inequality. That's why we must develop self-knowledge and self-respect and respect others as we want others to respect us. If we are Equal in everything which is an Ultimate impossibility to achieve, except for the One Supreme Being/Bearer- Who is always was, always is and always will be- who is
Eternal- no beginning and no end- then we won't be Equal at all. We are only equal in our Oneness with the One Supreme Being/Bearer.

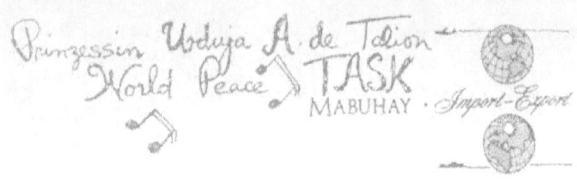

**Excerpts And Snippets On My
Self-Psychoanalysis. Self-Healing And Forgiveness**

27th September 1989   10-00 PM

At about 9-00 PM, I lay down with my son on his bed while waiting for him to go to sleep. He usually talks to me whenever we are together in bed.
'Is Jesus here in bed?' he asks.
'Yes, He's underneath your pillows,' I answer. This means that the large, black Crucifix with God the Father, God the Son Jesus Christ and God the Holy Spirit in the form of a dove, which belonged to my ancestors and which had been used for healing by my maternal grandmother, is underneath his pillows.
'You know, Mummy, if God holds the world with His hands, who knows, our house would be where His fingernail is resting. Does Gods finger gets a splinter?' My son asks me.
'What do you think?' I answer him with another question.
'Well, if he gets a splinter on His finger, where would He put the world so He can get the splinter out?'
'What do you think?' I continue to ask him with the same question which he does not necessarily answer to the point.
'Who holds the other planets? Does God hold them with His hands? I know He holds Earth with His hands', my son continues expressing his ruminating thoughts verbally
'What makes you think these thoughts. Did you learn them at school?' I ask.
'No, they just appear in my mind. God is coming into my mind.'
'Perhaps, it is better if you say a little prayer to Baby Jesus and Mother Mary and wish them goodnight. Then you can go to sleep peacefully, ' I say.

He stops talking and after ten minutes, he's asleep. I get out of bed, wash the dishes, silvers, pots and pans and start to write this short incident. So help me God.

**Excerpts And Snippets on My
Self-Psychoanalysis, Self-Healing And Forgiveness**

SPIRITUAL TREASURY

Please withdraw from therein-Spiritual nourishment, Spiritual strength, Divine providential guidance consisting of:
Holy Masses of intrinsic value
Holy Communions
Confession (Sacrament of Penance)
Holy Rosaries
Stations of the Cross
  Housefuls of laughters, smiles, songs, petty quarrels and pouts, domestic conflicts, delicious mental tastes of my home cooking flavoured with the tune of undying verses in my mind and heart, of faith, hope and Love, curried with the spicy memories of my childhood in the Philippines and of my teenagehood in Munich, West Germany.

Payable on demand to and herewith enclosed is also a £5 cheque from my thin bank account for the success of your benevolent cause for World Peace.
Also included are the "in Absentia" blessings of His Holiness Pope John Paul 11, and an "unofficially" approved moral support from our future King, HRH Prince Charles, who I spiritually pledge loyalty to, tempered with the spiritually-rational prayers from my Filipino Spiritual Director and 'friend Archbishop Onesimo Gordoncillo, Archbishop of Capiz, Roxas City, Philippines.
In addition, there are £3 million worth of Spiritual Bouquets consisting of Sampaguita, the national flower of my beloved Philippines with its mystical fragrance, of Her Majesty, The Queen's Roses from England, my adopted homeland and of Edelweiss with its aristocratic simplicity of Germany, my other adopted homeland. These are all illumined with the supernatural and sanctifying graces from the Almighty God and Lord of all Creations and Creatures, through the Holy Masses, Holy Communions, Holy Confessions, Holy Rosaries and other indulgences and prayers.
May be withdrawn directly from Westminster Cathedral and Westminster Abbey in London, Our Lady Queen of Heaven Catholic Church in Frimley, Surrey and indirectly, from the spiritual-mystical-atmospheric-ambience of my beloved country, the Philippines, the 'Land of the Morning' and the 'Pearl of the Orient

Seas,' as well as from the symbiotic-harmonious-oneness with the whole Creations of God, our Creator . . .for the Oneness of Divine nature and Human nature, for the coming of Gods Kingdom into this world, for the peaceful destiny of humanity and for the solution to the mystery of Life Everlasting. Amen.

Your spiritual-friend,

Princess Urduja A. de Talion
Urda von Deutschland
Mrs. Antonia Urduja Talion Roberts of the United Kingdom
Posted by: Antonia Roberts Jun 2 2005, 09:55 AM

To the German Counterpart of Antonia- known as Urda Talion -

My dear Urda!

You are my German-Individual-Self and I haven't met you for some while now and you are becoming a stranger to me. Don't go away, otherwise, I might become fragmented again. That little girl in me called Urding Talion is still intact while my present British Individual-Self called Antonia Roberts manipulate the actions, reactions and interactions of my present individual self- like an
Independent Variable in a designed experiment that should have internal validity and should be Beyond Reasonable Doubt. My dear Urda, you are the Dependent Variable that has got to be measured to see if the manipulations of the independent Variable who is Antonia has caused many changes!
Changes? Well, physically, yes, even emotionally, yes, but mentally...Oh no.. No changes! Mentally, I am always Urda-the German girl-woman and a little bit of the Philippino little girl known as Urding Talion.

Meine liebe Urda, kannst Du mir helfen mit meinem TMA 02 von SD226 Kurs vom Open University? Kannst Du Sankt Michaelskirche und Frauenkirche besuchen und zum Mutter Gottes Maria und zum kleinen Kinder Jesuskristus und zu den Heiligen Geistes beten, damit meinen Gehirn diesen Fragen vom
TMA 02 solvieren und antworten werden koennten? Ich werde mich ehriich sehr gluecklich daran...ich meine, Antonia wuerde sehr Dankbar sein zu Dir, liebe Urda! Ich koennte dieses Jahres nichts nach Muenchen fliegen und Urlaub machen. Ich habe kein genuegendes Geld zu bezahlen und spenden. Auch, ich moechte mich viel lernen, besonders mit SD226- Biologische Psychologie- Explorazion vom Gehirn und Nervoesen Systemie, damit ich meine Nervoesitaet verstehen und kontrollieren und konditionieren koennte.

Jetzt muss ich mich wieder anfangen zu lernen. Es ist in die Nacht, cirka 2335 Uhr: ich bin bei der Arbeit aber all Rezidenten in dieses Heim schlafen sie sich im Gemuetlichkeit. Es ist sehr stil, sehr leise, ohne "noise" (konnte die Uebersetzung auf Deutsch mich nicht erinnern). Ich moechte diesen Brief schreiben ohne Woerterbuch weil ich moechte mich sicher sein ob mein Deutsches

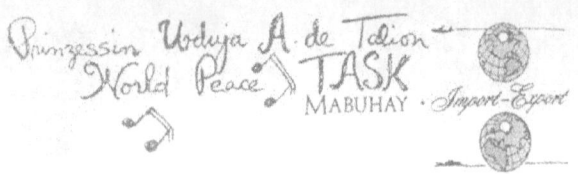

Kenntnis bleibt noch in meinem Gehirn. Nun muss ich gehen um die Medikamenten zu teilen.

Viele herzlIche Gruesse zu unseren Freunden und kannst Du fuer mich ein Opera im National Theater oder Deutches Theater sehen? Ich vermisse sie viel, ich werde daran denken weil Du bist im Theater werden sein. Viel Vergnuegen und alles, alles Liebe und Gottes Segen.

Dein Alter-Ego,

Antonia Roberts
11 Mai, 2005

Meine Liebe Urda ! (Mein Alter-Ego!)

Vielen herzlichen und herzlichsten Dank fuer Deine Hilfe. Es wurde sowie einen Transubstantiazion geworden sein...als waere die "jigsaw puzzle bits" alles untereinander das Bild eingeformiert haben wuerden sein. Meine liebe, liebste Urda, Du bist ehrlich eine Genie-sehr smart und intelligent !!! Gott segnet Dich!

Ich habe aufgewacht-getrauemt das Du National Theater besucht hast...und...tsk...tsk...tsk...Rigoletto gesehen hast. Muy bien, mi amada, Alter- Ego! Kannst Du dieses erinnern? Im Dezember 1966 hast Du und Urding Talion (die Kleine philippinische Prinzessin) mit WUS-World University Service, auf die Ludwig-Maximmillian's Universitaet in Muenchen in einen Seminar nach West Berlin teilgenomen hast, fuer eine Woche. Antonia Urduja Talion Roberts existiert noch nichts...nur Urda und Urding. Zweimal in die Nachts sind wir (8 Studenten von 8 verschiedenen Staedten) nach Ostberlin gefahren. Das wurde sehr abenteuerlich geworden sein. Einmal haben wir Rigoletto gesehen in dem Deutchen Stadtheatre in Ostberlin. Und dann, hatten wir gehofft, geglueckt, gelenken, gelaoht. gesungen und gegangen und mit allen Armen gelinkt miteinandem im Unter den Linden Strasse bis zum Brandenburger Tor I Hah...Du wurdest sehr, sehr Nervoes...ehrlich...allen diesen Studentenen von verschiedenen Nervoesitaet-Vibrationen ! Fuer Dich, das wuerde ein Traum in die Unwirklichkeit und eine Erfahrung in die Realitaet vom Lebens. Und, dann die andere Nacht hast Du Swan Lake Ballet mit Rudolf Nureyev und Margot Fonteyn gesehen ! Welche Herrlichkeit und Wunderschoen.

Jetzt, Antonia Roberts...ich denke daran und ich blinke meine Augen und konkludieren- Urda und Urding Talion sind auch Antonia Urduja Talion Roberts.
Drei Persoeniichkeiten in eine Persona. Mein Gott...Donnerwetter Gott nach mein das ist doch die Liebe Gott, mit Drei Personen ! Bin ich Gott? Nein, Gott bin ich nicht Ich bin nur ein kleines Voegelein mit ein Gehirn das prolifieriert gehabt worden hat.

Und, hast Du Deutsches Theatre besucht? Nein ? Oh, Himmel und Erde...ich habe Dich doch requestiert Deutsches Theatre zu besuchen. Erinnerst Du noch? Du hast mit Fritz ein Rechtsanwalt-Student auf die Universitaet Muenchen, im Deutsches Theatre im 1966 Faschings 'Thunderball' partie und Tanzen teilgenomen

hattest. Fritz hat Dir eingeladen und einen Kommilitonne vom Fritz-Karl, war auch mit uns. War das nichts lustig- ein kleines Voegelein-Maedchen mit zwei Herren als Eskorten i!! Das hat meinen Stolz eingeglueckt I!!

Ich habe auch neulich entscheiden, dass ich werde zuerst Kinder Buechen auf Deutsch, schreiben. Und dann, spaeter wuerde ich Novellen auf Englisch schreiben. Kannst Du das nichts vorstellen...oder...?

Nun, muss ich aufhalten einen Brief zu schreiben. Ich muss mich vorsetzen SD226 Kurs, TMA 02 Aufgabe zu lernen und vorbereiten und preparieren. Es muss zu unser Tutor nichts spaeter als 1 Juni 2005, sein werdet. Bete immer noch fuer mich.

Vielen, vielen Dank fuer alles. Viel, viel Liebe und Gruesse und Gottes Segen.

Dein Alter-Ego, die kleine Pnnzessm Urduja und das Voegelein
Urda von Deutschland.
14 Mai, 2005- Samstag

1-00PM   6 August 1994   Saturday

My Dearest Jesus!

It was about two or three months since my last Confession, therefore, I went to Confession today. I explained to Fr. Steve that just as I am about to find solution to my family problems, my mind always go back to December 1992 and the pains and wounds start bleeding again. His advice- I must be loving in a Christian way, like Jesus. Being loving does not necessarily mean that it has to be physical love, does it? Loving can be expressed in many ways.

I asked for Absolution and made a promise to work towards loving in a Christian way, like Jesus. So help me God and All.

Love, Tonie Roberts

'Be Loving in a Christian Way like what Jesus did. You have to work hard towards it,' Fr. Steve counseled me.
'I will try my best and I will make the effort, Fr. Steve.' I promised him.
'Do you want Absolution?'
'Yes Father, may I kneel in front of you for the Absolution and Blessing?'
'Yes, and thank you for the lovely towel you gave me. It was there when I came back from holiday.'
'Yes, Father Steve, I'll promise to learn to forget and I will make the effort to follow your advice.'

7-40PM   6 August 1994   Saturday

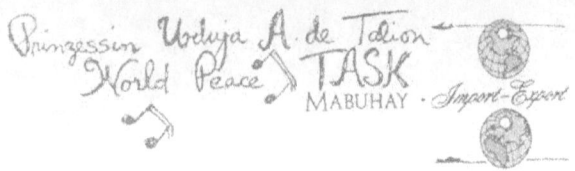

My Confession

Saturday morning. I needed to clear my conscience. My last confession was three months ago...long enough to affect the silence and peace within my soul. I felt pitch dark clouds hovering within my conscience, suspiciously bombarding into smithereens the Love within my heart, affecting the clarity of my mind and thoughts and destroying the piety and fervour within my being.
I met Elizabeth as I entered the main door of the church.
' Fr. Steve is already there, Antonia, she informed me.
' Thank you Elizabeth. Have a nice weekend' I said.

11-35AM   7 August 1994   Saturday

I feel like typing Fr. Steve's advice/counsel to me in Confession yesterday. The words keep ringing and echoing in my mind and heart, day in and day out, hour after hour on occasions.
' Be loving in a Christian way, like what Jesus did. You have to work hard towards it.'
I will imprint these words permanently in my heart and mind and I will gradually make the effort towards 'healing' the wounds inflicted upon me by the elements. I'll always think of what Jesus said on the Cross;
' Father, forgive them for they know not what they do.
Yes, I did promise to Jesus through Fr. Steve in the confessional, knelt in front of him for my Absolution. But, I will have to do it gradually and slowly, and so as not to be hurt too much, as in the past. I will have to maintain Space and Distance (physical, emotional and even part mental aspects) from my loved ones so as to be able to see clearly where matters went wrong.

I must philosophize that perhaps God allowed them to happen, not because He wanted them to happen (like all other illnesses such as cancer, etc.) but because their occurrences and implementations were part of Man's Free Will, which God does not interfere with. Also, perhaps these pains were/are necessary for me to atone for my past sins or disobedience to some of the moral laws within the Catholic doctrine. I have not been an angel or a saint in my past life- therefore, it's a chastisement of my spiritual being.... maybe for when I see God face to face, either in death or in a trance or maybe in a Beatific Vision while I am alive. Who knows what could happen

to me in the future, I could die tonight in my sleep or I could live a hundred years with my present body.

So therefore, Suffering cleanses the soul and gives wisdom to the one who suffers, as long as he/she accepts them in the name of Jesus and in union with the pains of Jesus when He suffered pain and death for us during His Crucifixion on the Cross, as our Redeemer. I am certainly learning and gaining some bits and pieces of knowledge and wisdom, despite all the pains, heartaches, degradation, and humiliations. They are, I believe, cleansing both my body and spirit and soul and conscience, and that 'Mens Sana Et Corpori Sano' would, who knows, we could be able to continue the continuation of obtaining more tangible solutions to this axiom.

Love, Tonie, Urda, Nene, Urding, Urduja, Antonia Roberts.

11-47 AM   7 August 1994   Sunday

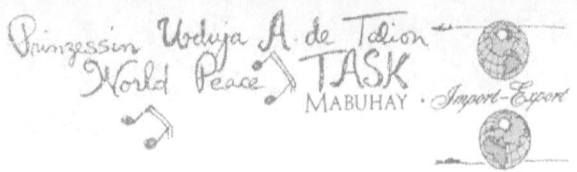

22 May 1996; Dear Father/ Lord God; Guten Morgen!!

I'm so concerned for my husband and his recurring chest infection...It's his fault! Many times in the past, I would tell him to see the doctor on the first few days of his chest infection.

' No..... I'm not a junkie, unlike you.' he would say.

He would wait and wait until the coughs get worse. His frequent coughs would worry me a lot. He believes in the Spiritualist Church Healing, being a Healing Leader.

I actually am not very keen about it, but I let him have his way. I would try to have healing sessions on my shoulder pains to be sociable and to find out what benefits I would derive from them. But I would not notice any difference so I would stop having healing and would concentrate on the Christian church healing, praying and going to the doctor.

I would reason out to him that the more he lengthens his chest infection without proper medications, the more susceptible his chest and lungs would become because that would lower the resistance of his lungs to heal.

'Rubbish' he would exclaim. He would get angry at me.

Now, he gets chest infection more and more often. But now, he goes to the doctor at the onset of his symptoms. What he does not want to understand is that his chest and lungs have grown weaker and weaker now due to his previous prolonged chest infections without proper Doctors' prescribed medications.

He gets temporary relief from his church's healing, but what healing energies are put within him to assuage his discomfort? Healing at his church does not necessarily cure but it just gives temporary comfort and well-being.

12 January 1997, Sunday, 6-40 AM

On Tuesday, 14 January 1997 would be 9 weeks since my last Depixol Injection. I have felt withdrawal Symptoms of various kinds, the worst being extreme headaches, or continuous migraine for several days which I've counteracted with Anadin/Paracetamol. Occasionally, I took at irregular times Largactil and Kemadrin. I have felt the depression, even extreme depressive desires to let go of myself and just expire in myself and go to Never-never-land by not waking up anymore- to just sleep forever and be with my Gernot, my first-love who died in February 1965, who died in his sleep while on a skiing holiday with his friends in Tyrol, Austria at the age of 25 years and a medical-intern. I was then at Harefield Hospital, England when this had happened. That was the worst-ever shock in my life that had ever occurred to me, worse than anything that had ever happened to me because at that time, I loved him too, too much that I lived solely for him then and for nobody else! He also had chronic hepatitis because of alcohol. I often remembered when Schwester Elia, my German adopted mother and I used to visit his sister's house then where he lived and we used have dinner with them, beer-drinking sessions while Gigi and Marion (6 and 4 years old) stayed with us in the lounge as we conversed in German. I was then only a passive conversationalist because my knowledge of the German language was still very little. But, I had to drink beer because I was given one and everyone else was drinking beer, except of course, Gigi and Marion. How I loved and admired these two beautiful and attractive blond-haired little girls. And when it was time for them to go to bed, they'd say 'Gute Nacht' to all of us and curtsied as well as offered each of us a handshake. That was a marvellous custom, which I fell in love with, much more so because at the hospital, we did also make use of a lot of handshakes and curtsies. These forms of greetings became second nature to me, so that even until now, I still occasionally 'pepper' some of my actions with either handshakes and/or curtsies, or maybe even both at times. I didn't count them and I didn't even bother about doing them, they just occurred to me as part of my second-nature. There were several Sisters and nursing students in the hospital who were of royal blood. I could write about these much, much more but right now, I must focus on my withdrawal symptoms...

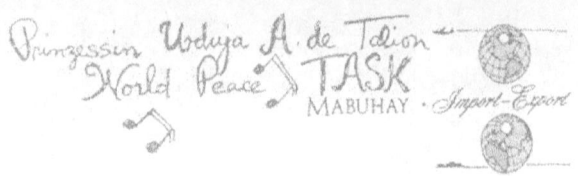

Sleep, sleep, sleep! As a night care assistant in my present world, I used to feel the real need to sleep, sleep, sleep. The elements and my family didn't understand me. But I believed that I really needed to sleep, sleep, sleep and sleep some more to drown and forget the unmerciful manners I was treated by the elements. I could not just accept everything that I had been subjected to by the elements due to misunderstanding and unawareness. It had been going on so.... oh so very long that I just had lost interest in coping to live. In fact, I was actually and simply existing, not living.... I just wished to go to Eternal Sleep and Eternal Oblivion and mingle with the Sun, Moon and Stars in the Heavens. Yes, they've always been my brothers and sisters and they've succored me many times in my grief. I've temporarily cut-off' my tangible and physical and outward objective relationship with my family in the Philippines as well as with my relatives and friends in America. I wished to just concentrate on my personal-individual problems- in fact; I've also temporarily excused myself from going to my Catholic church. I just limited myself to my individual-personal ways. I prayed a lot in my mind and in my mind and heart. I was always present in the activities, especially on Sunday Masses in Our Lady Queen of Heaven Catholic church. Yes, I just could not stomach what was happening to me, so I just Sleep, sleep, sleep so as to forget, hoping that Eternal Sleep and Eternal Oblivion would come to my rescue and embrace me and kiss me and take me along with them to never-never-land!! Yes, this was what I felt, this was what I felt would happen. I've just lost interest in all the everyday realities of objectiveness in daily life- I just didn't seem to know the differences between Sex and Marital Sex. I hated Sex....I hated my husband....he had manipulated my life and my ways. His Spiritual forces were very strong. They didn't understand me and I didn't understand them.

Bless me Father for my Human Folly and Human Imperfections, which somehow in one way or another resulted into Venial sins. My last Spiritual Confession was yesterday. I pray the whole of the My Simple Prayer Book everyday since a long time ago even before the birth of my 32 year old daughter. And I pray a lot more everyday- that's the Burden my Mother has bequeathed on me- Pray without ceasing not only for me and my family but for the whole of Humanity.

I am in the midst of writing my second book, aside from my job as a Night Care Assistant. The book is entitled- Lucifer's-Dream-Magic.

I have always been taught in schools and in college in the Philippines that Lucifer is female angel or female-archangel...the most beautiful and the most clever of all the Angels and Archangels in Heaven. That's why she was called - The Bearer Of Light. It was transubstantiated to me in November 1972 (as in my book) that the Triune God has Three male Divine Persons contained in the One Supreme Bearer in His Divine Nature and Divine Love; and that Angel Lucifer is Their Human Sister contained in The One Supreme Bearer in His Human Nature and His Human Love, the Essence of my Ex Cathedra Doctrine. How the One Supreme Bearer manifested Himself to Lucifer and to God the Father...how the Father created the Tree of Knowledge of Good and Evil, how Adam and Eve were created by the Father are written in my second book, etc. etc.

In another part- the descent of the Triune God to Earth to reconcile themselves, as was the Will of the Father; to their Human Sister Lucifer, who was already long time ago driven out of Heaven because of Misunderstanding on the part of the Father- Contradictory misunderstanding in mentalities and ways of thinking due to Individual differences. Through this reconciliation, it was noted from various prayer and spiritual books, that Jesus became Human, yet He was a perfect man. He never gave way to the imperfections of human nature. But, in my novel, the reconciled Lucifer had to semi-indoctrinate Jesus to the imperfections of human nature, as willed by the Father and the Holy Spirit.

It is very complicated to explain in a short story. The Father, after His recent visit to London with Jesus and the Holy Spirit, to search and reconcile with Lucifer and to invite her to come back with them to heaven. The Father had had a heart attack on their way back to heaven because His Being had partaken of the Impurities of Earth and Human Nature and the World. He was operated on by the Spirit Being of Dr. Christian Barnard- an open heart surgery done by the Spirit being of the doctor. Etc. There is a little sex in it but I promise to treat this delicate issue with refinement.

When Lucifer was welcomed in Heaven, Mother Mary told Jesus that Lucifer still got on her nerves; therefore could she remain in her holiday abode in Luna/Moon, until she could get used to having Lucifer reconciled into heaven.

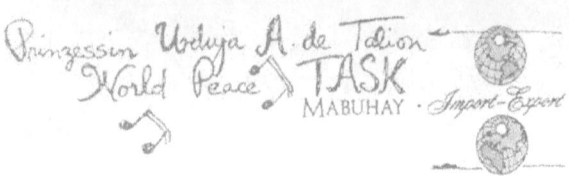

She was also uncomfortable due to the fact that some of her images venerated on earth show the serpent which was the symbol of Lucifer, being trod on by her. "Of course, you may do whatever you wish" Jesus replied.

In Luna, Mother Mary had a rehabilitation, medical and mental-health centre called the 'Identificatum Memoriam Sanum.' Spirit-beings from various constellations, galaxies, universes and planets, including Earth popped in and out of this centre. Meanwhile, Jesus and Lucifer popped in and out, with various identities in various parts of the Earth and other planets and continuum. Jesus wanted to transubstantiate human nature through the tutoring by His Sister Lucifer. Jesus wanted to be Human, this time with all the faults, mysteries, imperfections and human passion.

In fact, it was here in Luna's health-rehabilitation centre where Jesus noticed this beautiful princess- Princess Diana But, Dodd was always at her side, sometimes she was being accompanied by Mother Theresa. Princess Diana was being rehabilitated from Bulimia causing her occasional emotional imbalance. At first and on several instances, Jesus viewed her from a distance. But He was getting romantic notions and was developing human passions towards her. He consulted Mother Mary, Mother Theresa and many others. The last and the most helpful was His Sister Lucifer. It was a very long and intricate process of courtship by Jesus aided by Lucifer and the Holy Spirit, which resulted into a Romantic-Friendship, between Jesus and Princess Diana, which grew deeper emotionally and passionately... et al. There's a little politics in it, Paris, Rome, USA, etc. included in their adventures, etc. etc.

Please think of me in this venture and I'll keep praying for you to the One Supreme Bearer. May you be blessed. Thank you again.

Antonia Roberts

Bless me Fr. for I have sinned- my last Confession was months ago in Westminster Cathedral in London. I go there once in a while to visit, light candles, attend Masses and go to Confession. In the distant past, when I was gravely ill emotionally, I used to bring my own candles, bouquets of flowers and perfumes. I used to work part-time in Lentheric Morny Cosmetics when the children were young at school, hence the perfumes and colognes from the staff shop. I can even remember myself giving an expensive perfume to the priest in the confessional. I also used to go to Westminster Abbey, every time I went to the Cathedral before they started charging money for entrance to the Abbey. It was in Westminster Cathedral when I had an apparition of the Blessed Virgin Mother and also in the main Dome at Salzburg, Austria where I also had an Apparition of the Our Lady of Altoetting when I was still suffering from my post natal depression way back in the eighties and/or nineties or both. In fact, when I was very ill, mentally and emotionally, I used to go often to Munich to renew myself in the Catholic Churches where I used to go in the sixties when I was a student nurse in the German hospital in Munich. Also, Fr. Rowley and Sister Monica came to my Home and gave me the Sacrament of Extreme Unction, the exact year, I cannot remember.

My sins are: - just some occasional domestic quarrels, which may or may not be sinful but normal. Part of it is the lack of mutual understanding between husband and wife because of our individual differences and personality clashes. For these and all the Sins I have committed, I ask pardon and blessings from God and Penance from you, Fr John, through your Authority vested in you, in the ministry of the Sacrament of Penance within the Hierarchy of the Catholic Church.

I am very happy of the monetary donation to the Mission and I wanted to share my happiness with you, thus the German chocolates which I bought recently in Munich and which I hope you liked. That's my usual way. When I was a student nurse in the German hospital, the Nuns and patients used to give chocolates, sometimes money, hence one of my pathways. I am quite aware and somewhat familiar of how the Mission works. My uncle, may he rest in peace, was a Catholic Bishop in the Philippines and he was the Director of the Philippine Mission Society. He was one of those many Catholic bishops and archbishops who used to attend the PAX ROMANA in Rome during the time of His Holiness Pope Paul VI during the sixties. It was through the Bishop that I was able

to train as a German nurse in the German hospital in Munich, run and owned by the Francescan Third Order- a very rich and affluent religious Organization who were active in missionary work, especially in Africa. They used to help my uncle by soliciting benefactors for his mission appeals. He and several Filipino priests studying for their doctorates in the Colegio de Seminario de Filipinos in Rome, used to be invited as guests to the hospital. I used to take these priests around Munich for entertainment. One of them is now an Archbishop in the

Philippines and when the Bishop, my uncle died, who was also my spiritual confessor and adviser, I asked this Archbishop if he could be my Filipino Spiritual Adviser and he accepted. Everything was carried on through letters-mail. My adopted German mother, also a nun of the Francescan Order and was then the Medical Secretary to the Gynecological Department of the Hospital, the only nun who knew English, used to translate German letters from benefactors into English. I can still see myself typing some of the letters of appeals to the generous benefactors, whenever the bishop was a guest in the German hospital, for his schools, hospitals and seminaries in his Diocese.

Thank you, Fr. John for Everything. I also wish to ask you to think of me and pray for me and my World Peace Task on Mental Health, once in a While.

Love in Jesus, Antonia

Looking Up...

I die!

In peace and in joy! Or shall I say, I pass away? It is more ethical to say so.

But, why am I in hell? I thought that peaceful and joyful souls go to heaven- Or, perhaps, being an atheist and an ignoramus, I just don't know the difference between heaven and hell. More so, I don't feel dead.... I don't feel like being a soul.... I feel so alive; body, soul and spirit with all the faculties of my individual self, before this transformation had occurred. Am I really transformed?

Am I really dead? I feel lost and confused.... Perhaps, I am just having an attack of Alzheimer's disease. I remember having been a carer in a care home for vulnerable adults.

I want to cry, but no tears wet.my eyes. I want to shout, but my voice is choked. I want to sleep, but sleep seems to forsake me!

Forever and Another Day

Today is forever. Tomorrow is another day, and is a great blessing from the Divine Source and Almighty Power that sustain us all- the world, nature, animals and humans.

Last night was an iota of time and eternity; a tiny glimpse of the fulfillment of our heavenly desires and of our dreams; dreams and desires that were nurtured in the Garden of our Minds and Memories, and in the Garden of our Hearts, Passions and Emotions.

Last night was a dream, today is a reality and tomorrow will be a fantasy.... a futuristic-fantasy-world based on a loadful of realistic dream. Last night was old age, personified and symbolized by wisdom, and the dream of last night was realized by her magical encounter with Brother Death.

Today is a reality.... forever a reality because once we've implemented and executed our plans, actions and decisions within the boundaries of today, these are forever indented within our day to day Book of Records of Life. Tomorrow will always be a fantasy.... a futuristic-fantasy-world overwhelmed by realistic dreams. For whenever tomorrow presents herself to us, either with a sad mournful or smilingly happy face, she becomes today. Therefore, as the cliché goes – tomorrow never comes!

Right And Proper

'You, English, you always want things to be done right and proper...
'
'So, what's wrong about that?'
'Why can't certain things be left wrong and not do anything about it... at least, temporarily until it's the right time....'
' And when is the right time supposed to be?'
'Well.... well.... when you know it's the right time.'
'How do I know it's the right time?'
'Don't you know how to feel without making impulsive decisions?'

My Brain's Mind

I should feel it in my brain's mind and I should see it how my brain's mind works the process to be solved through activation by the neuroprocesses of the neurotransmitters of my brain. Then I know that I am alive, that my mind generates the solutions to the problems that should be activated both by the brain and the nervous system.... then I am aware that all the body needs to do would be to follow what the brain has directed my senses to execute.

Wings Of My Spirit And Of My Mind

The Spirit and the Mind have Wings and there's no limit to the Intangible and the Abstract that can be recreated Tangibly and Objectively (as the Walt Disney Philharmonic Hall in Los Angeles- the City of the Angels) for the enjoyment, self-development and the widening of the Spirits and the Minds of those who visualize and kinesthetically sense them. Alternative Metaphor: Music is Art and there's no Art without Music. They are like Husband and Wife, each compensates for the shortcomings of the other, in the name of Love- the Great Healer of many ills, pains and heartaches with the passage of Time, to the fulfillment of our Destiny.

**What I Wanted,
What I Got,
What I Want Now.**

When I saw T185-Practical Thinking short-course in the Open University brochure, I knew I needed to take this course.... my neurotransmitters agreed to tell me so. I have already graduated with Honours from the University of Life- my subjective-inner-worlds,

I have had eight letters of acknowledgement from the Vatican- from His Holiness Pope John Paul 11 and Pope Benedict XV1, 1 letter from The Queen, 5 letters from Prince Charles, 2 letters from Ex-President Cory Aquino, and 1 letter from Ex-President Fidel Ramos- both from the Philippines, 1 letter from the deceased King of Jordan, 2 letters from the then Prime Minister, Mr. John Major, et al. They would prove the authenticity of my Honours degree from the University of Life of Subjective Thinking.

Now, I need to balance that with this course- T185-Practical Thinking, to activate the growth of my objective-outer-worlds. And, to make it more worldly-wise and objectively-honourable, I am presently reading for a BA/BSc Health and Social Care (Honours) degree. And, hopefully, too, afterwards, a Masters degree in Philosophy, and God willing, if I am still alive- maybe a Doctorate degree in Theology!!

Good Heavens Above.... what would I do with all these degrees? I would present them to St. Peter when I would have to knock at the entrance-door to Paradise. I am executing the fulfillment of the Prophecy of Our Lady of Fatima for World Peace, part of my ancestral heritage, and, I believe that I have already experienced an iota of eternity in the heavens.

Now, I am looking for the stairways that would enable me to descend to this world of objective-reality. I have already finished studying the courses, K100- Understanding Health and Social Care and SD226 Biological Psychology, Exploring the Brain and my neurotransmitters decided on T185-Practical Thinking course, for me to study.

PT 24: Working at your best

When operating at my best, I am like a mango tree and a ukulele. The mango tree has grown and still grows in the garden of my ancestral home in Calolbon, Philippines. The house is now gone, ravaged by intermittent typhoons and storms, but the mango tree is still there. My second ukulele has been given to me by my father five years ago when he was still alive. It's now decorating our lounge at home in Surrey. My father has been dead for three years. I miss him very much. I have been his darling daughter! He has been a great man- a lawyer, a barrister, a politician, a writer and poet, an orator, even a singer---a man of varied talents and potentials. In the end, he has lost himself to Alzheimer's. The wood of the ukulele has come out of a mango tree. I take the ukulele to the residential home where I work as a night carer, play it to entertain the residents with old-time favourite music. The mango tree bears heart-shaped, sweet and juice-fleshed, yellowish-red skin when ripe which I enjoy eating at leisure. It sways and bends with the wind and rain- from left to right, upwards and downwards, when the wind is strong and the rain is heavy, as in a storm or a typhoon. However, in the end, when the tempest has subsided, the mango tree stands up tall and straight and majestic, like a Queen. Both practical and idealistic in heart and mind, does a tree have a mind?

Part I: The metaphor

It means that I have weathered so many storms, typhoons and other calamities in my life. It highlights the fact that my idealism nurtured with some sense of practicality has carried me through my pathways- through Faith, Hope and Love and Trust in the Divine Providence of the Godhead. It conceals its source- that this idealism has been and still is a family tradition; also my present moral problem with my mother, the physical scars has become emotional and mental scars to-date- those which she has inflicted unto me as a child, relevant to the emotions of anger and jealousy, I, being her eldest daughter and a fathers pet. Its concealment is also my unconscious desire to activate and potentiate my ancestral and parental heritage (genetic and acquired) such as my father's intelligence and idealism, his strength in character and in his moral and spiritual values, his positive approach towards the subjective and moral values of individuals that have been dented by

materialistic outlook and objective desires to enhance objective goals without being backed-up by moral and spiritual principles. I have forgiven my mother for the physical punishments she has inflicted upon me as a child- by believing that moral principles and values are above emotional values and feelings. But, the emotional scars and pain, which have been non-existent within me until now, have resurfaced from my mind they come and they go. Her past anger has diffused within my memory, so that as a child, I have feared her. I have been often nervous in her presence. I have floated above me and have viewed myself as a child in our ancestral home and garden- by the mango tree playing the ukulele, which my father has gifted me when I have been ten years old, together with the instruction book for playing it.

Part 2: Evaluating my Metaphor

My strongest values are- Faith, Hope, Love and Trust in the Godhead delineated through from within my past personal experiences- moral and spiritual values. I adhere to sharing myself- not just my personal-objective-outer-self but also my subjective-inner-worlds catalysed through the divine providence of the Godhead.
This sharing is symbiotic- which means to me that even if I don't expect rewards for what I share, the Divine Master will know my motivations in sharing myself and the reward will be bestowed upon me by the Godhead, in spiritual values though some of my sharee do reciprocate what I've shared with them.

The benefits from being like my metaphor-the ukulele and the mango tree- are Joy, Happiness and Strength in character. Most people share what they don't like anymore- say, their cast-off clothes given to Oxfam and Help the Aged, their illnesses and their pains, etc. However, I share what I also still like, ex. I share 1/3 of the juicy, sweet ripe mango that is my viand for my meals, I share happy thoughts, smiles and laughters and happy memories. They multiply in my pathways, principle wise, I share part of the best that I still like and not my cast-off personal items. Share the good and not the ugly.

Some limitations from being like my metaphor- ukulele and mango tree. I cannot fully utilize just yet my ukulele and mango tree metaphorical inner-world and landscape and attune my vibrations

and rapport to the razzmatazz of this younger, ultra-modern-world because of my other duties and commitments- families, jobs and money. Also because as Jesus said, the time is not yet come but I am happy as I do things slowly but surely.

Part 3: Mapping

I showed the drawings that capture some of the strengths and weaknesses of my metaphors to my husband. My husband did not comprehend it, he belongs to a different world as I do, in matters like this. We, however, have common interests, which we share together and we compromise. What I've debated with my mind are- which is higher in value- moral subjective principles or emotional objective principles? I think moral principles outdo emotional value or even emotional intelligence because moral principles are more attuned to the Godhead whereas emotional intelligence is man-originated and man-made. Love and forgiveness go hand-in-hand and I have forgiven my mother long, long ago and my mind is at peace in that matter, although the emotional scars still resurface from my mind, occasionally. But then, I think of Jesus when He first said: Father, forgive them; for they know not what they do these words are healing words, which spell SUCCESS!!

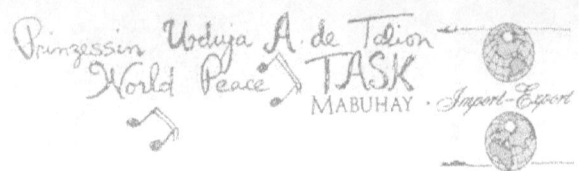

Perspective 8: Portfolio Task 23- The Basis of Rapport (Part 1)

Miscommunication is considered as a failure of rapport, according to the course material. But, failure is a stepping-stone towards Success . . . if we don't fail, we don't succeed . . . according to David Taylor's book, The Naked Leader Experience, David Taylor being the guest speaker of the Mayoral Reception hosted by His Worship, the Lord Mayor of Woking, Surrey, on behalf of the Open University Alumni.

Yesterday afternoon (10-11-05, Thursday) I've attended the Over Sixties social club. There were six of us sat around one table in the hall. I was pondering on whether I could attend the above mayor's reception in Woking, Surrey. I had travel problems. I asked the lady sat next to me if she knew H G Wells Centre in Woking. She was pleased to be asked and proceeded to explain how to go there, from the train station. I told her about the mayoral reception that evening, in the centre.

"Are you going?" my friend, Sheila, sat at the other end of the table, asked me.
 "I want to go," I replied

It turned out that she was invited, too. Right then and there, we made the decision to attend the reception together. My husband would drive us to Woking at 6-00 pm and would pick us up from Woking at 10-00 PM. The party conference-reception was a huge success. The High Sheriff of Surrey was elegant in his uniform complete with the traditional sword. David Taylor's speech focused on inspirations messages on how to make the best of your inner-self to your outer-self and be motivated by looking for your inward-riches within yourself; cultivate and potentiate them to attain your goal of success... whatever success meant to you.

Sheila-who I've got a very good rapport with; and I, used to work together at nights, in a nursing home for two years. She was the Sister-in-charge and I was one of the carers, but we worked together in the same unit. We worked hard but we infused our own sense of humour in our work, which blended together and which camouflaged our fatigues into positive mental attitudes. The foundation that generated the development of our rapport were self-respect and respect for the other, trust and a sense of equality

between two people and amongst the members of our team. Sheila and I shared and practised that.

Another individual who I had and have a good rapport was/is Moira, an Irish lady, the proprietress of the residential home for 9 residents where I work now, for three nights, as a carer, and where I worked, on and off since 1994. Moira is a people's person, according to my husband. Indeed! Moira and I have now, a sisterly-rapport with one another. However, when we talk about work, we are both professionals. Outside work, we are like sisters. We respect and trust one another. She is very clever and I am more intelligent than she is. She acknowledges that and respects me for it. But, we both act silly at times, together with other staff and that generates laughter and fun and enjoyment from the residents. I sing, I act and make impressions, I recite poems and verses-sometimes those that I composed and could remember that instant, play my ukulele and sing again and we all have fun in the home, more when than not. Both staff and residents are like a closely-knit family.

I grew up in an environment whereby my father- a lawyer and politician- have emphasized all the time the importance of public relations as a way of life. I must have grown-up with it but without the awareness of it. People have commented about it.., but I never noticed it within me. It was an inherent talent within me, which acted out very naturally from within my genes, as different from those character traits that are trained and acquired. Through backward reflection and guided visualisation of my growing-up years in the Philippines as a child, and in Munich, West Germany as a teenager, I have had so very, very many friends... international friendship became a way of life for me.

I've worked as a night auditor in the Sheraton Heathrow Hotel, in The Gloucester Hotel near Earls Court, London and in the Sheraton Park Tower Hotel in Knightsbridge. I was then, always the centre of attention without trying to find it because I generated a natural rapport as the basis of international-friendship. I also worked as a front-office cashier in the than newly-opened Skyline Hotel now Sheraton-Skyline Hotel near Heathrow. Modesty aside, I was then the most popular employee there. I joked (my style) with employees from cleaners to general managers. They patterned their styles with mine, with my sense of humour, while chatting with me in my presence, when were not busy. All these above places where I

worked were Homes to me. And, in my memory lane, they were my "homes. I generated rapport- the genes that my father had gifted me. Public relations was his term for it. I also worked as a bookkeeper/accountant in a Jewish Import-export family firm. The owner/director would go down to my level to share, my sense of humour and blended it with his. He regarded me as if I was his own daughter. I also had a German adopted mother. "Mutti" was how I addressed her. She was a Third Order,
Francescan nun as well as a nurse, in the general hospital where I trained as a nurse in the sixties. I was only 17 years old then She adopted me, unofficially, and really and seriously assumed the role of a mother. Some of my German friends became my adopted sisters. Looking inwards in myself, I have so much, so much more subjective wealth than these, but I must retain some for my future autobiography which I have already started but put aside, momentarily.

A person who I have no good rapport with.
Sue- the manager of the nursing home where I work two nights each week, as a care assistant. Nothing goes right when I go to see and consult her. She views the contents of my messages, back to front or inside-out, most of the time, Sometimes, Sue denigrates and humiliates me even in the presence of others. She can be nice to me, at times. I've made the decision to contact her as little as possible and only when it is very necessary. But, I understand her situation and I don't hate her at all. It is my principle not to hate any person because I believe, that each person is the temple of the Holy Spirit of God...to hate the bad deed done, instead. It's funny how the owner/manager of the residential home treats me like her sister whereas the rapport between the manager of the nursing home and myself is of a misunderstood-warfare.
A very profound resource for psychological and psychoneurological research. I've recently finished SD226-Biological Psychology- Exploring the Brain. I've noticed that there are some bioneurological phenomena that have relevance to some of the concepts, ideas and activities being dealt with here in T185.

I am the ukulele and a mango tree when I'm working at my best. I am also an angel when I am learning well. I'm also a Sparrow (Spatzlein- a tiny sparrow) the name I was given by my German friends in the German hospital where I trained as a nurse in the sixties. I still live like a sparrow though, even until now. My

metaphors for myself are conceptually blended (Fauconnier and Tuner, 2002). They are all inter-related to one another- there's joy, freedom, music and abandonment to the divine providence of the Godhead that generate happiness in my mind and heart.
What am I like? I am what I am and I am nobody else but 'ME'.
My identity and my individuality are very important to me.
I appreciate honesty with a childlike rapport, in a person.
I dislike people who like to be me, but have hatred and envy for my personality traits that they want for themselves, who want to be better than me and with the wish to trample on my feet as their ulterior motivation, instead of being grateful for my generosity to them.

But, there are younger persons who would like to be like me with genuine sincerity with no desire to degrade me. I tolerate and I don't dislike them. Instead, I smile inwardly to myself because I know, they will never be able to be like me. Younger persons don't have the wisdom of the older generations. I inspire and encourage them to cultivate their potentials and be the best of whoever they are and of whatever they can be with themselves. In fact, I have one young African girl work-colleague who is presently studying K100- Understanding Health and Social Care which I've already passed, because of me, Many of these younger persons who are work-colleagues of mine come to me for advice.

The mango tree bears fruits- these fruits are my children and those colleague-friends of mine who had been inspired by me and are making contributions for the betterment of this world that we inhabit. I am happy to be an invisible 'role-model'.

Perspective 8- Portfolio Task 25, Ideal Projects

A perfect team project for me in which the structure, dynamics, climate, etc. were letting me operate at my best, would be my present family- my husband of 68 years, my daughter of 29 years living in Nottingham, my son living in Southampton with his fiancée, both of them aged 24 years and myself; 61 years old, living with my husband in our house in Frimley, since 1975.

Mabuhay- a Filipino word which means Long Live! and Welcome! - Is the name of our structured semi-detached house...I love her very much; she is my English roots and my destiny continues here. . I cherish her, she is the compilation of my conceptual-blended-image a house of Love, Joy, Music and Forgiveness! She's got a life of her own. She radiates energy, awakens and potentiates the talents within me and mine. The intensity of the climate within her varies with each season and the weather from day to day. Now that our children have already moved-out from our house, my husband and I have created and formed a lifestyle that blended with our past and would blend with our future individual needs, wants, wishes and desires, taking into consideration our human imperfections and human follies.

Our daughter's room, now houses our computer, scanner and printer, and is an informal office for my husband's duties as an executive member of the SNU- Spiritualist National Union. Informal in the sense that our daughter's double-bed and her exercise-bike and her other persons articles still decorate the room. Our son's room still houses his bed and his other personal articles, some of my books, study and course materials with the OU. And, of course, the master's bedroom which is overcrowded but is very important to us. An additional conservatory for my personal memorabilia is unique and sacred to my mind and heart And, of course, the porch, lounge, dining area, kitchen, the bathroom and toilet, the back garden with a shed for my husband's DIY paraphernalia and the front garden, the drive, the garage and the car.

The computer, printer and scanner are very important items to both my husband and myself a distant healing tutor and an assessor in spiritual healing, they are a must. As far as I am concerned, they are indispensable for my studies with the Open University. They help us and our children to have constant communication with each

other as a family, even if we live apart and we pursue our own work and interests, not just for our own individual satisfaction and self-fulfillment but also for helping the community in one way or the other.

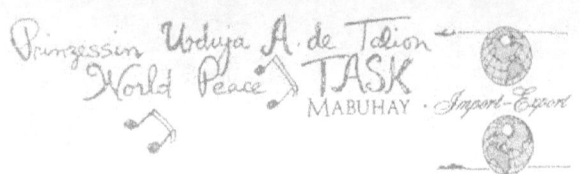

Some Of My Homework with the Open University, Course T185: Practical Thinking

Portfolio Task 18- Eliciting Your Coding Of lime
Portfolio Task 19- Locating Your Time line(s)
Portfolio Task 20- Working With Time

Eliciting Your Coding Of Time:

The past.... the past is noisy, uncontrolled and unfinished. Internally, my past is still my present, very old memories have consolidated my personality-fragmentation. I would travel down memory lanes many times and the black- and- white, silent snapshots become colourful and vibrant with life. I have stitched-in within my present, the black- and- white threads of my colourful and intricate past experiences.

I regard the colourful and intricate networks of my past-life as the time-foundation and a time-resource of strength, courage, moral principles and determination of my present pathways and struggles to solidify and unify my fragmented persona.... of my inner-worlds. I have had to go back time and time again, into my past-lifetime etched within the memory-lanes that I have traversed when I was a child in the Philippines and a teenager in Munich, West Germany. That would be the fifties and the sixties when the world was young and quieter. The colourful events intermingle with my sadness, grief and sorrows, love, joy and happiness within my time-lines of these two-intercontinental-dimensional-continuum.

Space and Time have gifted me with the will to live, strength and courage in my struggles, to love and be loved, to share myself and multiply myself in the act of sharing-generously and genuinely in God's name. I can depict part of me in my husband. I can see my younger-self by looking at and knowing my children- they are me! I have multiplied my persona-I have achieved a multiple persona and more than that, I am my children and my children are the younger, ME! I am unique- a gift of Space and Time, of my Time-line. I am independent, yet I am also interdependent upon my families and friends. I am Whole and Wholesome-happily and satisfactorily integrated to and within the strata of society.

The synaptic neural transmissions have produced action-potentials and the short-term memories of my present-time-line-coding have been consolidated into long-term memories within the hippocampal-areas of my brain. My glass is inundated with possibilities and the spring-water of possibilities have poured-in continuously and its limited content have been overfilled by limitless- possibilities that can only be determined by my mind's-eyes being a visual-receptor. Kinesthetically, I feel all these passing-circumstances like a video-movie on a television-screen or like a technicolour-dream in my transient sleep. My mind's eyes have to put a stop to the continuous-flowing-in of possibilities.... and I would have to choose which possibilities to cultivate and potentiate because my limited brain-power and intelligence would not be able to provide the 'Space' for them.

However, Time and Space could be obtained from the Godhead.... I must pray and search for Space in my spiritual-nature within the divine-human-continuum of my lifetime- to my Godhead and Spirits of my loved-ones, including the Spirits of my long-long-time-royal-ancestors in the bygone era. They owe me my heritage and gratitude for my travails and my insistence on struggling to survive so as to fulfill the pathways they have delineated for me in my future dimension of life.... the life-dimension that would transcend Space and Time, nature and reality, science and metaphysics that would solve the chaos created by Love and Hate, morality and immorality, and of superfluous contradictions- so as to be able to generate and create Peace in our Hearts and Minds, not only for the older generations but also for the Youth of today who would have to shape the dimensions of 'Time and Space' in the foreseeable future of tomorrow ....!

Locating My Time-line:

My memories of the past, consisting of two variations- one in the Philippines and the other in Munich, West Germany way back in the fifties and the sixties- and memories of my future here in England, or maybe, even internationally are arranged simultaneously in front of me and behind me. I see very vividly and feel kinesthetically my past lives- ex. When I am ten years old in the Philippines,
I am kneeling for two hours on a float dressed as St. Bernadette Soubirous, kneeling in front of the statue of Our Lady of Fatima, I am processioned around my hometown. And, when I am twenty-

two years old in Munich, West Germany, I am performing Filipino dances for my country through the International Students Club in the University of Munich, where I have been a part-time language student. I have transubstantiated the tangible memories of courage and determination to visibilize and tangibilize my dreams of becoming a successful published writer, a few years from now.

I have not anticipated any problem in viewing my past in front of me. However, I discover that this strategy creates nebulae within my efforts to succeed as an international-writer in my future. The past-strategy involves religious practices coupled with superstitious-beliefs which are of contradictory natures but which my mother adheres to despite my father's opposition to them. This illogical-strategy creates confusion in my already nearly-confused mind. Confusion builds-up nebulae in my thinking. My past in Munich, West Germany as a teenager has been tangibly and visibly-guided by my German-adopted-mother, who is a Third Order Francescan nun. Her motherly- guidance on my behalf is pure and unadulterated love and affection. Having two 'mothers'- my biological and German adopted mother, reflect a wider outlook in my mental and emotional perspectives and in my expectations for my future. But, these glorious expectations carry intricate burdens and unheard-of-complexities that besiege my mind.

These are my Time-lines- my past in front of me and my future behind me. My present is towards the middle, constantly moving and viewing my past and future which monitor how I would cultivate and potentiate my concepts and corresponding activities to achieve my future goal- that of being a successful, published international writer.
Working With Time:

In working with Time, I have to choose Approach 3- Editing a Time-line. The location of my time-line is in the Philippines, during my childhood way back in the fifties and my love- hate relationship with my mother. One incident have happened one night at home when I have been crying so very hard, for my mother. I have missed her so much and I have been wanting her physical presence to enfold me affectionately in her arms despite the fact that my grandparents were pampering me, so I would stop crying. My mother had been in church, attending to church activities allied to the CWL-Catholic

Women's League, as she has been its president. I have been crying for two-hours non-stop.

When my mother has arrived home, I have started to be happy, thinking she would enfold me in her arms and kiss me. But I have been mistaken.... instead, she has gotten angry at me and she has pinched me so hard, several times on my arms and on my buttocks. Pinching me has been a punishment my mother has given me several times on various occasions, that I really have feared her. And, these have generated and built-up within my system a nervous-fear and a love-hate relationship with my mother. It has been to my father and to my grandparents that I always turn to for my love and affection-needs which also has developed jealousy within my mother towards my father and my grandparents.

James and Woodsmall (1988) have suggested an activity of 'floating above your time-line, so that you could see the entire continuum of past, present and future below you....'
I have done this exercise several times and as I have been floating above the surface, I have felt good.... good that I am not with my mother anymore.... and good that I have not inflicted this punishment to my two children.... good that I am past all that.

'Now, I must float back in the time- in the 'now' and then go back again in time and pick-out a memory of the past that has made me very happy and I must relive that experience.' I have done it. Those have been the times when I have performed Filipino dances in several audiences in Munich, West Germany in the sixties- and then, I must go back to where I am- in the 'now'.

Then I have floated above my time-line all over again, and I have noticed that my past, future and present have different degrees of brightness and joy, continuously moving-about, sharing themselves and adding more brightness and joy to themselves. I have tested myself and I have felt dissociated in my thoughts, feelings and emotions. I have felt good and the darkness of my past from my mother has been forgiven (for after all, she is only human.)

And, in an associated sense of thoughts, feelings and emotions. I have felt the impact of brightness and joy in my Life having been generated from my own children of the 'now' of the present

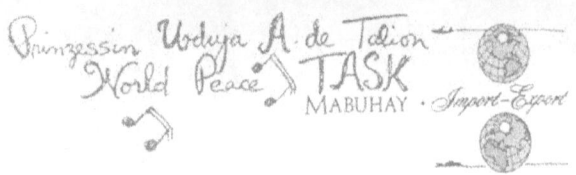

circumstances in my life. (Resource 29, James and Woodsmall- Editing a Time-line)

Portfolio Task 1: What is it like when you are learning well?
Portfolio Task 2: Finding metaphors in different areas of the world around you.
Portfolio Task 3: Identifying metaphors you yourself use.
Portfolio Task 4: Setting clear outcomes for the course.

PART 1 REPORTS:

Task 1: What is it like when you are learning well?

1) I become an angel flying to the seventh heaven while searching for the pathways I need, my mind could hear melodies of joy and self-satisfaction. AS an angel, I must assess my capability to fly- good, better, best or bad-, what are my tangible and intangible resources of Strength and Courage to undergo a
Search for the elusive seventh-heaven for as I fly higher, I can visualize that the higher and unattainable it seems and feels to me. And there are Obstacles that abound on the way such as limited time needed as imposed in the search but, once the seventh-heaven is reached, is an unselfish goal, motivation underpinning my search- such as sending out melodies of love and joy to the other angels in their ordinary residential continuum.

2) I become a poet creating and composing my feelings and emotions, as well as my other ideas and concepts, into poems and I feel high and elevated into space and unaware of the boundaries of Time.

3) I become a young-me, way back in 1964, climbing the Alps of Wankbahn in
Garmisch-Partenkirchen, Bavaria, until the top where the Cross was planted within a confined space. I was with my cousins and we were wearing our new leather-high-heeled-boots, which were novelties for us, perhaps some spectators were watching us with curiosity and a smile. And, as we stood by the Cross amidst the snowy-white surroundings, I sang- Greenfields- Once there were Greenfields, kissed by the sun, Once there were valleys Where rivers used to run.

4) I become a mother-eat lovingly nurturing her kittens with tender-loving-care.

5) I become a saint lovingly being embraced by my Lord Jesus Christ and an ambience of Peace pervades within my heart and mind and in my surroundings.

6) I relive my experience way back in 1998, when my husband and I were the only two passengers in the first class of a British Airways flight from Manila to Hong Kong, being pampered by the stewards and stewardesses. But once we arrived in Hong Kong, the first class was filled with Chinese passengers going to London.

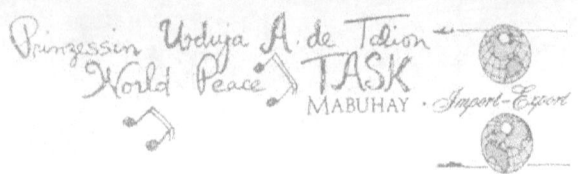

Task 2: Finding metaphors in different areas of the world around you

1) I travelled around the world in search of a loving wife, only to find that what
I was looking for was embodied in the woman patiently waiting for me back home.

2) Laugh and the world laughs with you; cry and you cry alone. (Proverbial metaphor learned at school and very common)

3) Distance makes the heart grow fonder. A proverbial metaphor, if lovers have to be apart, either because one party needs to travel abroad to perform a duty- the separation intensities the emotional love generated within both parties.

4) Friends are like melons, to find a good one, you must a hundred try.

5) My love is deep as the sea, a part of a song, mysterious happenings and mysterious creatures and unidentified wealth abound in the deep blue sea comparable to my love.

6) Age creates no barrier in matters of education and love.

7) His looks freeze me and his smiles make me soar to heights.

8) Arbeit macht das Lebens suess-sweet und das suesse Leben Sauer. Work makes life sweet and the sweet life, sour.

9) This go hand-in-hand with the proverbial metaphor that says- The Germans live in order to work, whereas the British Work in order to live. (Die Deutchen leben um zu arbeiten und die Englischen, arbeiten um zu leben)

10) "Ibon man ay may layang lumipad, Kulungin mo at pumipiglas..." (A bird has the freedom to fly, incarcerate it and it will struggle to come out of its cage.) Part of a Filipino song about the Philippines under the conquistadores and lately even under the Martial Law Regime of the then President Marcos.

11) El Sol, La Luna, Las Estrellas, Los Nubes y El Viento son Hermanos y Hermanas de Nuestros... (The Sun, the Moon, the Stars, the Skies and the Wind are our Brothers and Sisters...)

12) "Ang hindi marunong lumingon sa pinanggalingan, Ay hindi makakarating sa paroroonan"... (One who does not look back from where he/she comes from, won't be able to reach his destination) Tagalog or Filipino proverbial metaphor.

Task 3: Identifying metaphors you yourself use

1) Candlelight Flames Endure- my life has been surrounded by candlelights- their flames, gentle and mysterious! Their tangibility is deceptive, being attributed and characterized as weak, ready to expire with the slightest gust of wind. But, subjectively, I perceive them as my life's strength and endurance because their foundation lies not upon objective materials, but upon the Love of God that fills my body, mind, soul, intellect and spirit. That's why they had stood the test of time, of sunny and stormy weather, of peaceful and tempestuous climate, of health and of sickness, in war and in peace. Learning well is
Endurance by Candlelight.

2) Prayers can move mountains, supplanted by Faith and Love.

3) More things are wrought by prayers than this world dreams of- Foods for thought in my religious studies as a young student in the Philippines.

4) Knock the pub on the head. My daughter's metaphor, which means she'll quit her part-time job in the pub.

5) "To Beautify the Non-Existent in Nature is to Create. .
To create non-existent Beauty needs Wisdom. ..
And to beget Wisdom is to Beautify in your Mind and Heart
And create what is Non-Existent."
A poetic metaphor that I composed when I had my post-natal depression way back in 1978.

6) Pray without ceasing . . . this does not mean that one has to kneel and recite prayers from prayer books all the time. It means that we can consecrate all our thoughts, words and deeds to God

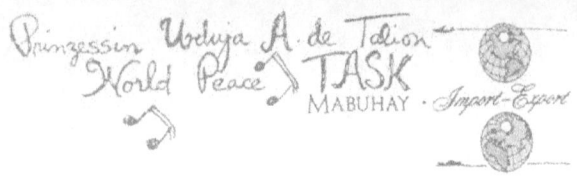

when we wake up in the mornings and again when we sleep at nights.

Task 4: Setting clear outcomes for the course.

1) To further develop my personality-growth so as to be able to understand the world and the environment surrounding my pathways in life.

2) To be able to think practically amidst the western world where metaphors are very important issue of usage in local, national and international decision- making in short, to be able to Objectivize my already Subjective conceptualisation of my mentality so as to be able to understand well and solve mental health problems due to diversity of cultures in our societies.

3) To change my Dinosaur outlook (out-of-touch and very slow-moving) into that of a swiftly-flying sparrow nurtured by the grace of God's Divine Providence.

4) Learning well is sharing generously, not only of material things but also of some aspects of your personality, principles and ideas. Sharing generously is symbiotic way of learning well, it is two-sided, the sharer or the giver gets a feedback from the receiver, in some form or rather, such as happiness and joy, if what is shared generates these emotions from the receiver. Symbiotic learning through sharing creates a larger world in our minds and hearts. If the motivation for sharing is genuine and positive and unselfish, the giver not only gets an objective feedback but also subjective feedback from one's guardian angel and the spirit-world.

After I have read 4 Portfolio Pan 1 on Perspective 1 submissions, I have indeed concluded that I am a Dinosaur (very out of touch with the Objective world and very slow-moving.) But, I hope to improve my next Portfolio, especially in my presentation and tune in my subjective-mental-wishful-thinking into Practical
Thinking that is the aim of this course, TI 85. I have never been aware until now that the English language is littered with metaphorical concepts and expressions. I was enchanted by the views mentioned in the 4 submissions of Perspective I, Part 1 and marvelled at how very carefully they were presented in the written form, as compared to mine, which was haphazardly-presented,

(before my improved version) my views were limited, fiction-like and impractical. In fact, that's one of the reasons why I am taking the short-course, A172-Start Writing Essays to help me improve my academic presentation of essays and assignments. Some reasons for my limitations are-

1) My age, being 61 years old- when one reaches this age, the mental alertness slows down, this has even been confirmed by my GP.

2) On top of that, I have developed a 'set' way of dealing with life and circumstances surrounding it and to 'unset' that way, is to be 'open to change' which I've also taken, also a short course with the OU.

3) So I hope you will bear with my slow, limited and unusual ways of presenting matters relevant to the questions and ideas in this course which I am beginning to like and am slowly enjoying, which I first found out as very, very confusing. And, I hope to imbibe some positive outcomes from studying this course, TI 85 and to activate the dinosaur's mental agility within me, hopefully...!

Reflecting On The Course Ideas-

Mixed Feelings, Emotions, Understanding, Sharing and Healing-
Experiencing
Writing those Portfolio Tasks, of my implicit-subjective-worlds, to be integrated with my explicit-objective-worlds, so as to generate actions and interactions through genetic-potential-potentiation and energy-inputs/outputs, for my goals-achievement-programs, is like Baring myself in the Confessional-box and in the Psychoanalyst's couch. Long-term and short-term memories are consolidated within specific brain structures, and they are like three-dimensional movies parading before my mind's eyes.

Perspective 1-Sub-session 3.2- Comparison, categorizing, analogy and metaphor- 4 modes with obvious differences.

I, vaguely, remember in 1992, when Mr. John Major was running for Prime Minister versus Mr. Neil Kinnock. In one of his speeches, he compared Mr. John Major as Prime Minister to the category of the 'plumber. I immediately wrote to No. 10 about the illogicality of

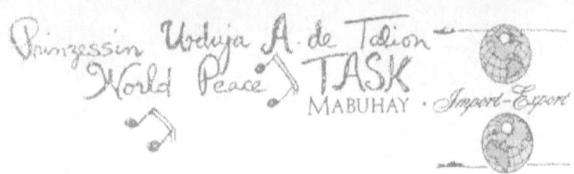

the comparison- a prime minister to a plumber. I reasoned out that a Prime Minister is an Architect and an Engineer of a Nation, who needs to have a high degree of intelligence to create, beautify and rebuild a Nation's inner-beauty and stability. Whereas, a 'plumber' needs only a short training on manual dexterity and skills. Also, that a Prime Minister, as an Architect and Engineer of a Nation, may need years to execute and complete his tasks, whereas a 'plumber' may need only an hour or more, to repair the plumbing system of a building. However, due to some 'unavoidable circumstances Mr. Neil Kinnock resigned from his candidacy as Prime Minister to the Labour Party.

The comparative metaphor used in the speech-comparing a prime minister to a plumber-showed a lack of 'deep-thinking'. No comparability was assumed here! Comparison generates actions and interactions towards the fulfillment of your dreams and goals, through it, you can view where 'your weaknesses lie and comparatively, your strength manifests before your very eyes.' And. mathematically, you evaluate how your strength can conquer your weaknesses so as to earn your 'crown of laurels.'

'Rhetoric' and 'artificial', and figurative application of words include metaphor and analogy'- John Locke quote- great British philosopher- 1690.

He should have been a mathematician and/or a physicist, instead of being a great philosopher, if he viewed 'the art of rhetoric as artificial and figurative application of words' used to 'insinuate wrong ideas, move the passions and thereby mislead judgment, and as indeed as perfect as cheats...' as well as 'rhetoric, that powerful instrument of error and deceit.' (Extract from Resource 2: A short history of metaphor.)

Mine: The art of rhetoric in philosophy is wisdom coated with cream and honey, to provide the intellect with a sense of reasoning that would transcend the heavens and to experience an iota of eternity in the continuum of Time and be at Onement with the Divine. And, indeed, passion magnifies the aura of man's soul to merit a place in Paradise- be it heaven or hell- for hell can be a paradise for those who are dammed on Earth.

Associated or Embodied Thinking or being emotionally involved; Dissociated or Disembodied Thinking or emotionally detached but with Empathy.

Doctors and Nurses are trained to empathize but not to be emotionally-involved with their patients. In fact, medical ethics dictate that surgeons are not allowed to operate on their own family members. Although, healing is associated or embodied thinking and action, yet, a space has to be maintained between the healer and the patient. That space generates respect between each other. Empathy enables the healer to feel and understand what the patient is suffering from, but with disembodied philosophical thought through reason.

Reason is embodied. We manifest explicitly the principles and ideas of reasoning. The same neural and cognitive mechanisms that monitor and control our perception and motion, also define our conceptual networks and modes of reason.

Michael Apter (2003). ' Personality is dynamic not static: we are more like dancers than statues.

'Michael Apter argues that the ability to move freely and appropriately between these states (Different personality rooms) is probably a very healthy sign, and being stuck in one 'state' is probably less satisfying and less desirable.' (Perspective 2, 122, Different types of personality and personal style.)

Mine: Self-knowledge generates awareness on the limitations of human near-infallibility, or so it seems, aided by modern technological inventions. Also of the limitations of a person's abilities, capabilities, talents and ingenuity, as affected during growth and personality development. Unconditioned upbringing from birth to maturity is healthier, as compared to conditioned-upbringing. In the former, the individual explores events and circumstances, by trial and error techniques; all his genetic and acquired potentials, and then develops the best within him to the full; whereas in the latter, the internal and external worlds may become fragmented first, before both can be made whole.

Metaphor: Unconditioned-upbringing awakens self-knowledge.

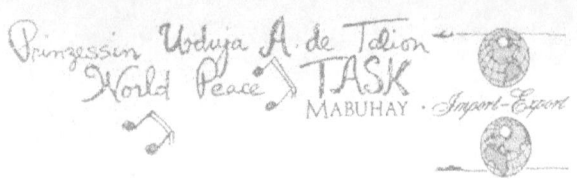

Addendum: ' The way you are as an adult, is, of course, determined partly by your social and economic context, partly by your inherited genes, and partly by your life experiences.' How very true I (Reference: Perspective 2, Session 1, Introducing Differences, Sub-session 1.2- Difference is a key-resource and Beyond the underlying differences.)

Perspective 5, Session 1, Sub-session - 1.3 Projection as an emotional minefield.
When my two grown-up children were at school, I would wait for them after classes, together with the other mums at the school gate. We used to discuss our children's follies, and oftentimes, I would hear them say – 'I know exactly how you feel!' Silence used to be my reply. Inwardly, I would philosophize- ' How could they know exactly how I feel when they are not me...?' Eventually I got fed-up and I scorned at those words.

I have observed that here in the West, the process of identification and projection are common ways of dealing with daily life activities. Example: mothers identify their feelings and emotions with other mothers and project their feedbacks towards other mothers. When identification and projection are carried on a positive viewpoint, good results could ensue. But, if they happen within a negative stance, identifying with a very angry person harbouring anger within oneself and then projecting this anger to some innocent person, then that's when the problems arise. And, if often repeated, that's when - projection and identification become emotional minefields.

Conclusion:

This course on Practical Thinking, T185, was a stepping-stone for me in externalizing my internal potentials, following my own individual pathways through verbalization. I was a late-starter because I was doing my ECA (End Of Course Assessment) for another course. Confusion shocked me right at the very beginning. But, my tutors were very understanding during the online conferences and I was able to adjust and continue until the end of the ECA. Nowadays, I am in constant lookout for metaphors everywhere- television, newspapers, radios, conversations, letters and books, etc. Here are a few that I 'dug out through to within my head.'(a) If you want to keep growing, you need to maintain the environmental conditions for growth. (b) ' Target was set for the developing countries and not for the developed countries.' (Ref: Both from TV interview on Climate change. 3/12/05) (c) Leadership must have human values, motivations to your people, clarity of direction and should be connected to objective-reality. You should keep learning about yourself and you must be comfortable in unknown territory.' (Ref: W Interview.) I thoroughly enjoyed writing without 'word limit' glaring before my very eyes and I believe that, I am a stronger person-objectively, for having taken this course. And, I have found the continuation of the 'stairways' that would enable me to descend to this world of objective-reality, which I was looking for, as I've mentioned in Part 1 of this
ECA.
References: Course T185, on Practical Thinking with the Open University. Part of my ECA (End Of Course Assessment.) Printed without the Tutor's corrections.

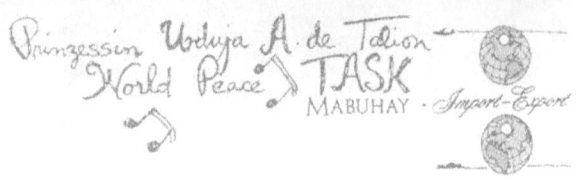

THE LEARNING PLAN

1) What do you want to learn from this course?

I want a junior outlook of being a beginner all over again, thereby reproducing a new individual-mentality that is of my own creation- a conglomeration of various phases of principles and attitudes that I have developed in the University of Life (according to my NVQ Level 3 & 4 in Care and Manager's Award trainer and tutor) incorporating Changes to slant to the Objective Realities of the younger generation of adults and children. I want to cultivate the virtue of humility to counteract my arrogance and I want to be able to find out how I can realise so many of my dreams and visions in some foreseeable future, as a role model in one way or another.

2) Which skills do you want to improve during this course?

To be able to improve and continue to develop my writing skills and slant them towards the objectivity of a multicultural society. Also, to unblock my writer's block and to be able to develop more skills and strategies in studying for higher studies in the future.

3) What else do you want from the course?

To be able to clearly visualise and identify my strengths and weaknesses, my past, and my present, so as to create relevance to my current-present and present- future goals and objectives.

4) In this box, write about how your previous experiences of work, education and everyday life have given you skills and knowledge to help with this course.

I started writing poems at the age of nine years. In high school in the Philippines, I was good at essays and was a staff member of the college publication organ. I won a bronze medal in a provincial competition for poetry and won first prize in an elocution contest in college.
I had a children's story published when my first child was only six months old and I had several star letters to the Editor in various newspapers and magazines, published. My mind is used to switching from one extreme to the other but sometimes, I get

confused because I am nervous, I want to find a strategic-therapy there to.

I have not completely deskilled myself but I want to sharpen and activate and update these skills that I still possess. I want to consolidate and prioritise my talents and potentials so that I do not only enjoy them but that I would be able to build up a decent amount of financial security, for my children, to be able to build a house for my mother in the Philippines and to be able to fund and continue with my research through personal development, on Mental Health, a small contribution for World Peace.

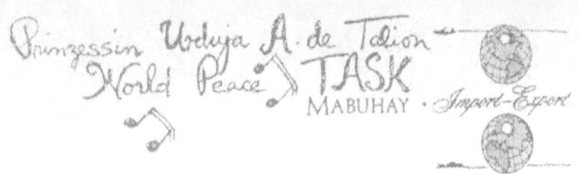

From: 'A U Roberts' -------
To: --------------
Cc: "---------"
Sent: 25 April 2004 10:35
Subject: TMA 2, Open to Change

My Goal: The one goal I aim to achieve within this coming year is to become a successful published writer and poet.

How...? Why...? How and why did I choose this particular goal?
I had been married for 31 years with two children, girl of 28 years and a boy of 23 years. I have done so many varied things in my life and have had so many small successes as a writer and two poems published. But, I chose to be a full-time mother and housewife when the children were born, all throughout their youth. I've enjoyed those years including the difficult challenges...one being post-natal depression in 1976. To be a successful published writer and poet someday were always foremost in my mind, next to the needs of my children and husband. Now is the proper time for me to commit myself to my writing endeavors.

Who will help me?
Courses K100, Y152 and Y154, The emphasis on Essay writing will help to unblock my writer's block Entering short story competitions in Women's magazines. Encouragements from my husband and children.
The sheer love of writing as motivation factor.
My mother's prayers and mine for my success and my religious beliefs.
I should restart reviewing, studying and rewriting my two unfinished novels hand-in-hand with the study courses with the Open University.

Who will hinder me?
My unorganised lifestyle.
My insecurities and lack of confidence once in a while.
I find it hard to start communication but once I have started, I lose my self-control and I just talk.

What can I do to help myself?
Watch plays, operas, operettas, ballets and musicals in the theater once a month.

Read and study paperbacks novels and short stories in magazines.
Physical exercises every morning for 5 - 10 minutes and combine it with meditations and prayers impact on my own and others' times.
My husband would complain and get neglected by me or he would be pleased or maybe a little jealous of me.
I should become financially better-off. My families in the Philippines would be happy for me. I could realise one of my many dreams to have my mother's house rebuilt in our hometown in the Philippines.
I would 'grow big' in the eyes and the estimation of my relatives, friends and town mates in the Philippines.
But I would still work two to three nights as a Care Assistant! I don't want to relinquish this job and colleagues at work, doing this job keeps my sanity at bay and work is an integral part of my home life.
Network of support I can draw on.
God, Angels and saints and spirits in heaven through prayers, meditations and good work of sharing.
My membership with the UNA-United Nations Association, London...Cllr- Catholic Institute for International relations.
Moral and spiritual support from my friends in the Our Lady Queen of Heaven Catholic Church and in the Women's Fellowship in the St. Peters Church of England Church in Frimley, Surrey where I live.

My life has been a series of constant changes especially in my work . . . as for example, within a period of thirty years in my life, I have had approximately twenty jobs of which I am proud of. Other women would be proud of having been divorced several times in so many years, (I don't blame them) but I am happy and proud to say that I would be celebrating my 30th wedding anniversary on the 22nd March 2004. But within these thirty years of my marriage, changes are the prevailing ingredients that make my life happy and sad, stormy and sunny, stupid and wise, laughing and crying . . .and most of all, worth living for! An understanding mind and heart are worth mentioning, too.

My underlying values and principles that are worth living for are- the nobility of my aim of the goal that I am striving for . . .to become a psychiatrist. But I know I will never become one because I have no desire to study the full medical course and then specialize in Psychiatry, which is the proper way to do it. Therefore, I need to find a second best goal that would help me with my research on Mental Health- Mentalities, Attitudes, Feelings, Emotions and Nerves- Diversified Nerves that impair mental health when misdirected and not understood.

"Psychology is the answer . . ." my GP advised me.

I have actually not changed the Indent of my persona, I am still a whole and I am solid, only the circumstances in my life have changed. My gratitude to Carl Gustav Jung on behalf of the elemental-Indent of a persona. There was a time when I became fragmented in 1976, when I have had post-natal depression after I gave birth to my eldest child. My self-prescribed therapy was to travel to where I had been before and visit my friends and family. I travelled to Munich, West Germany several times to rescue my German-identity (I lived there in 1963-I967.) I am now aware of my German-European identity as distinct from my Filipina and British images. I also travelled to the Philippines many times with and without my family of four(husband, wife, daughter and son) and solidified my Filipina identity. And of course, my British identity is made up of universal components, which I have immentalitated, inculturated, acculturated and interdenominationalitated.

I see myself now as undergoing a period of transition. My mind is rejuvenating and my heart is embracing the Objective realities of

this modern era in conjunction with my set of values and principles. My heart will always be a Filipina, my mind is German-European and my nerves are British/English. I also know now that I have to be objective in my approaches without transgressing on my subjective persona. I also know that I need an up-to-date university degree!

Now, I am studying course K 100- Understanding Health and Social Care with the
Open University- one of the best things that's happening in my life. I hope to achieve a BA/BSc degree in Health and Social Care and providing that I am successful, I shall continue studying for an MA in Philosophy and Psychology- my favourite 'mental/emotional - reservation-suites!' And, who knows . . .maybe a PhD...? But that would be several years hence, still somewhat unrealistic in accordance with my present states of mind and heart. However, I have a solid background, the active potential qualities and experiences to a set of values and principles of good practice and an unselfish and noble goal to support me in these objectives. Also, I need to do these with the Open University because I am self-funding and I need to maintain my job as I study.

And what has maintained me. . .? Love and prayers, Pain and Sufferings in my mind and in my heart . . .not necessarily in my body. These are the light and the clouds that sustain my journey towards getting closer to my God, who gives me a resilient mind and Joy in my heart and soul! And, two Deaths in my family- that of my Father who died of Alzheimer's Disease and of my younger Brother, who died of a Cardiac Arrest- in the year 2002. I didn't cry then, but now, I keep crying whenever I think of them.

"Where did I go wrong?" I question my God with utmost Humility. An Endless Silence always follows my questionings! But, I know I must go on... And, I known I will succeed... And, I know I will find the answers...And.....

Option 2... Reflect on your past experiences and where you are in your life at the moment. How do you see yourself now? In what ways have you changed over time and what has changed you?

My life has been a series of constant changes. In my thirty years of marriage, changes are the prevailing ingredients that make my life happy and sad, stormy and sunny, stupid and wise, laughing and crying . . .and most of all, worth living for!

Who am I? I am a person with many facets- mother, wife, writer, poet, student, care assistant . . .a has-been psychiatrist student nurse, filing clerk, night auditor and front office cashier in three four star hotels near Heathrow Airport, waitress, typist- bookkeeper- accountant in an Import-Export Jewish family firm. When my children were at school, I worked as casual in Lentheric Morny cosmetics factory, as a crew member in McDonalds, and as a factory worker in Johnsons Wax. I even became a voluntary helper in a nearby hospital and in a social club for elderly people . . .entertained them with my songs as I played with my ukulele. I always treasure the good and happy memories in my past jobs and hopefully, the various skills, too. As a Carer- my present job, I have passed my NVQ Level 3 in Health and Social Care, my NVQ Level 4 in Care and Manager's Award. The theories and practices in my jobs have enabled me to cultivate and nurture the qualities of patience, humility, creativity, determination, open-mindedness, sensitivity and continuity.

I see myself now as undergoing a period of transition. My mind is rejuvenating and my heart is embracing the Objective realities of this modern era in conjunction with my set of values. My heart will always be a Filipina, my mind is European- German and my nerves are British/English. I also know now that I have to be objective in my approaches without transgressing on my subjective-persona. But, of course, I still make big mistakes even until now! And I know that I need an up-to-date university degree. That is why now, I am also studying Course KIOO- Understanding Health and Social Care with the Open University- aside from this mini-course, Open To Change- one of the best things that's happening in my life. I hope to achieve a BA/BSc (Hons) degree in Health and Social Care. I am self-funding, and I need to maintain my job as I study.

There was a time when I became fragmented in 1976, when I have had post-natal depression after I gave birth to my eldest child. That was the critical point that triggered the continuity of changes in my life's pathways. My self-prescribed therapy was to travel to where I had been before, and visit my friends and family. I travelled to Munich, Germany several times to rescue my German-European identity (I lived there in 1963 until 1967.) I am now aware of it as distinct from my Filipina and British images. I also visited my family in the Philippines many times, with and without my nuclear family of four (husband, wife, daughter and son) and solidified my Filipina identity. And, of course, my British identity is made up of universal components which I have immentalitated, inculturated, acculturated, interdenominationalitated and synchronized with my German-European identity. I have no option but to change for the better to uncover the missing-links of a wholesome and solid persona. That is why, I am doing a personal research on Mental Health-Mentalities, Attitudes, Feelings, Emotions and Nerves-Diversified Nerves that impair mental health when misdirected and misunderstood, my humble contribution to this multicultural society.

And, what has maintained and sustained me . . .? Love and Prayers, Pains and Sufferings in my mind and heart. These are the lights and the clouds that sustain my journey towards getting closer to my God- who gives me resilient mind and Joy in my heart and soul!

"Where do I end?" I question my God with utmost humility. An Endless Silence always follows my questionings! But I know I must go on . . .And, I know I will succeed, And, I know I will find the answers . . .And, I know I'll meet many more changes...And.....

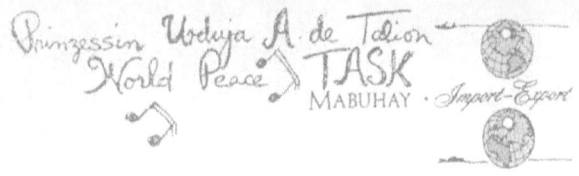

Open to Change, TMA 2

The one goal I aim to achieve within the coming year is to become a successful published writer.

How . . .? Why . . .? How and why did I choose this particular goal?

I have had so many plans, visions and dreams that I have had aimed to achieve but I had never made a commitment to choose one particular goal. I think I am a scatterbrain . . .maybe I am still a scatterbrain. In 1965, I wanted to be a singer in a nightclub . . .not necessarily to become a professional singer. And in 1973, I worked as a night auditor in the Sheraton-Heathrow Hotel. I used to empty the cash tills and audit the takings in the coffee shop, the colony room, the colony bar and the pub called The Footlights. The pub manager and the barmen were friends of mine from the other hotel where we've worked before. They used to call me, Eartha Kitt and they've asked me to sing on the stage several times and I did. They were besotted by me and my songs. They've got friends who could give me an audition . . .and who knows . . . I could be another Eartha Kitt! They would exclaim. I took singing lessons from an opera singer in 1966 while I was in Munich, West Germany. . And, who knows, Indeed! I would motivate myself. I became hopeful and bought music scores around London. I practiced my singing again, privately. My emotional life at that time was in turmoil . . .I had no emotional intelligence at all!

What do I want out of life- fame, money or love? If I became famous and rich, would I be able to cope with fame, wealth and success? What is fame and money without love? my mind and heart argued. I chose love. Therefore, I rejected the invitation for a musical audition. Love finally came knocking at my door and I got married to an Englishman in 1974.

I had been married for 31 years with two children, girl of 28 years and a boy of 23 years. I have done so many varied things in my life and have had so many small successes as a writer. But, I chose to be a full-time mother and housewife when the children were young. I've enjoyed those years including the difficult challenges . . .one being post-natal depression in 1976. To be a successful published writer someday was always foremost in my mind, next to the needs

of my husband and children. Now is the proper time/stage for me to commit myself to my writing endeavours.

What will help me? What will hinder me?

Help:
Course KlOO with the Open University. The emphasis on Essay writing may help to unblock my writer's block.
Entering Soon Story competitions in Women's magazines.
Encouragements from my husband and children.
The sheer love of writing as motivation factor.
Visits to theatre once in a while
Reading paperback novels,
My mother's prayers and mine for my success and my religious beliefs.
Hinder:
My unorganised lifestyle
My Insecurities and lack of confidence once in a while
I work 5 nights a week as a care assistant.
Impact on my own and others' times?
My husband would complain and feel neglected by me.
I would barely have time for socialising.
No more shopping sprees to while my time away.
If I succeed as a published writer and become a full-time writer, I should become financially better-off My family would be happy for me. I could realise one of my many dreams to have a house built for my mother in our hometown in the Philippines.
I would grow-big in the eyes and estimation of my relatives and friends from our hometown- many of them already in various countries outside the Philippines. I could also buy a small studio-type flat for me where I could continue to pursue my career as a Writer . . .our house is too overcrowded! But I would still work, perhaps 2 or 3 nights as a care assistant. I don't want to relinquish this job and colleagues at work; doing this job keeps my sanity at bay and work is an integral part of my extended home-life.

Support I can draw on.
My membership with the UNA- United Nations Association in London
CIIR- Catholic Institute for International Relations in London
Open University- Courses I am taking, K100, Y154 and Y1 52

They keep my brain alive and busy and help to unblock my writer's block and regenerate my mental processes
My friends in the two care homes where I work.

Title: Discuss the kinds of evidence that are relevant for evidence-based mental health practice.

An evidence is a proof that will enable us to believe or do something. An 'evidence-based' mental health practice is based on this proof. It aims to help service users/survivors to realize their aspirations for mental wellbeing and mental fitness so that both body and mind could work harmoniously and function effectively. And to achieve mental health and wellbeing in 'evidence-based' mental health practice, our studies underpin the philosophy of Holism which is the integration of both body and mind, taking into consideration that all parts of the person as one. The practice consists of treatments, therapies and philosophies that have produced positive results through studies and research. There are two types of 'evidence-based' mental health practice; the notion of 'expert' evidence and 'experts in experience'. 'Experts' in evidence are usually professionals in mental health practice. Some of them are psychiatrists, psychoanalysts, psychologists, mental health nurses, psychotherapists and social care workers. They acquire their knowledge through studies and research.

Knowledge is information in action (Gray, 2003) and their knowledge is called professional knowledge. Experts in experience are usually lay persons such as parents and those who have had first-hand personal experiences of mental distress or who had been service-users/survivors, themselves. Their knowledge is known as lay knowledge. Some of these professionals may be both experts in evidence and experts in experience. They may be mental health practitioners, themselves. They are participants in evidence-based mental health practice. The gathering of evidence fall under two categories- the traditional hierarchy of evidence and the spectrum of evidence. The first category believes that a special kind of knowledge-evidence is superior to others. But, why traditional? Because the treatment had been considered the best for generations, had been originated by experts in evidence, had been published and had been supported by experts. The latter considers that there may be useful evidence from different sources of knowledge, depending on who controls them. The two approaches in the hierarchy of evidence are: 1) Qualitative research- aims to analyse, understand and develop the subjective aspects of the inner feelings, emotions, words, images, music, art and the spirituality that people attribute to their life-experiences. They closely analyze human behaviour and cognate future behaviour.

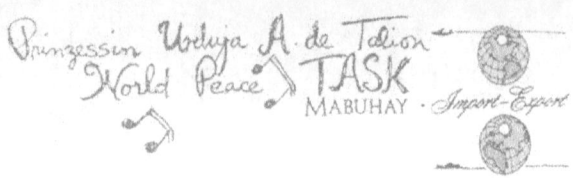

They include depth-interviews, close and detailed observations, and yield rich and unstructured effects. 2) Quantitative research is objective, logical and stands to reason, deals mainly with finding out data on a large number of people or animals such as statistics, surveys, questionnaires, random-controlled trials, random-interviews. Rod Davies, principal of Orient Century Market Research, Asia pointed out that the former focuses on the right brain and the latter deals with the left brain. When the right brain creates problems for us, the left brain scans it's reasoning power to get us out of trouble. Quantitative and qualitative research go hand in hand. It would be unfair to decide which is the best because objective quantitative data can offer a structure to the evaluation of subjective qualitative data.

"Evidence, especially in mental health is always changing .. .how and why . . .and, are these changes in 'evidence based' mental health practice for better or for worse?

It would promote a better understanding if I were to give a brief summary of the development of the mental health field through to the present 'evidence-based' mental health practice. Critical evaluation of the past can strengthen or weaken the process of going forward from the past through to the present and unto the future.

The Poor Law Act of 1601 advocated caring for social outcasts in parishes, and in 1630, workhouses were built. In the 17th century, these workhouses became 'commercially-run' madhouses, which treated the wealthy-mad differently from the impoverished-mad (Bushfield 1996); the start of caring for social outcasts as a business enterprise. In the 18th century, the religious orders set-up charitable voluntary asylums, The Lunacy Act of 1845 provided massive public asylums to house the so-called mad or lunatics, irrespective of as to whether they were mentally ill or simply had learning difficulties. These asylums became experimental learning institutions' for new medical treatments for the insane. One approach was the 'medicalization' of 'moral treatment'. Porter (1987) had explained the concept that if insane people were handled more humanely, they would behave within reason, but that they should, nevertheless, be 'trained' to be normal. And mental health practitioners afforded them with both medically scientific treatments and compassionate-care. A vague start of evidence-based mental health practice can be delineated here. By the 1960s, primary care policies became explicit, gradually started to be delivered by general practitioners and mental health teams in the community. Evidence-based mental health practice in mental health nursing was given emphasis and importance. By the 1980s, those large mental institutions with extensive areas of land were sold and vacated. The trail and demented elderly men and women were placed in nursing homes and /or residential homes. Private homes mushroomed in various communities.

Caring as a job was gradually upgraded with the compulsory training for carers through NVQ levels 2 and 3 in Health and Social Care and NVQ level 4 in Managing Care with emphasis on evidence-based practice in mental health and in various areas of healthcare. Outpatients' clinics, insulin therapy and

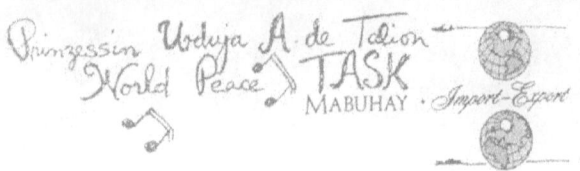

electroconvulsive therapy (ECT) were developed in Britain with the introduction of community care. New drugs associated with mental illness were discovered in France and in the U.S.A. Some approaches based on Sigmund Freud's work (1856 - 1939) became an evidence-based mental health practice. And with the New Labour government, evidence-based practice both in medicine and in mental health became popular and compulsory, a strategy to modernize the healthcare system.

But, sometimes, because of the constant change in circumstances occurring within nations, due to the diversity of nationalities, cultures, traditions, beliefs, values, principles and religions, certain traditional hierarchy of evidence practice needs to be temporarily set aside to give way to new contemporary treatments and therapies, but not to be completely forgotten. Why? Because in the course of times, they may be usefully integrated and incorporated within the new contemporary treatments and therapies to produce more effective outcomes. Some of them are- the Electroconvulsive therapy (ECT), psychotic drugs injections, talking therapies and these changes in evidence-based mental health practice for better or even Random Controlled Trials using Cognitive Behaviour Therapy (CBT). A person undergoing ECT is given general anaesthesia and electrodes are applied onto his head. I have had several ECT treatments in the distant past and instead of suffering memory loss, as some service-users pointed out, I have developed resiliency in my memory faculty within and have quantified my memory-space in my mind and in my cognitive faculty within my nervous system. The electrodes applied onto the head cause convulsions, therefore, could be dangerous. It had been reported evidentially that a certain number patients died while suffering convulsions during ECT treatments but the benefits outweighed the disadvantages. Psychotic drug injections can be beneficial for those suffering from post-natal depression, medically named as 'puerperal psychosis'. 1976 was the birth of my first child and I was a victim thereof. I would have had suffered strokes on several occasions but the timely injections of this psychotic drug prevented me from having strokes which would have paralyzed some parts of body. Certain cultures in India and in other parts of Asia and Africa, especially amongst the women are against talking therapies. Is it because these women are supposed to be demure and secretive of their feelings and emotions, and it is considered vulgar to broadcast them? Anyhow, in the West, people are encouraged to talk and to

expose even their innermost secrets in some techniques called depth-interviews and random interviews . . .both qualitative and quantitative research, respectively. Here's an example of a Randomised Controlled Trial using a brief CBT-
(Cognitive Behavioural Therapy) Intervention. (K272, Module 2,Unit 7, p.l5). CBT is motivated by the concept of people being able to learn skills in solving new problems and counteracting unidentified nervous fears. This research chose 422 schizophrenics. They were split into two groups- the control group whose routine care remained unchanged and the intervention group who had brief sessions of CBT for two to three months. It was found out that the intervention group had improved their schizophrenic symptoms, suffered less depression and gained more insight. However, further investigation into the long-term results indicated that those who stopped having CBT and taking their medications relapsed with even worse consequences than the control group. Would this be an evidence of success or failure in the ever-changing evidence-based mental health practice? But, are these changes for better or for worse? Change is a very expensive activity which involve a large amount of financial and human resources. But the resources provided within the mental healthcare is limited. For example, those inmates in the public asylums that are non-existent now were let loose within the community under constant surveillance and close scrutiny by the community mental health teams. Many of them are unemployed and live on meagre benefits and are not mentally fit enough to live financially and morally independent lifestyles. They have a greater demand for financial and human resources than those in psychiatric homes. The New Labour government is envisioning a Utopia in the healthcare field with insufficient financial backing to fund new projects. Instead of smiles of satisfaction and contentment from service-users/survivors in evidence-based mental health practice, more complicated problems arise and the phase of living is becoming a rat-race that causes deeper mental distress to service-users/survivors. People live longer now and the constant demands to the healthcare community teams are causing tremendous stress both to the service providers and the service users. Labelling is a bad habit of the system in this society, and those labelled as mentally ill are getting more and more distressed...psychosomatic-distress. Dementia amongst the elderly is rampant. What should we do? We have not even found solutions to past and present problems, yet, more changes are implemented by the government in the healthcare system with the aim of

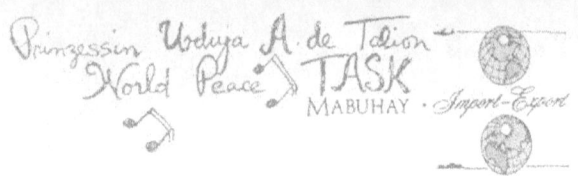

modernising the system. Modernisation in evidence-based mental health practice is under-resourced, chaotic and utterly irresponsible!

We can now understand how and why these changes had impacted upon the mental wellbeing of men and women, both young and old, male and female and children, most especially. Evidence-based mental health practice underpinned by the experts in evidence, experts by experience, the traditional hierarchy of evidence and spectrum of evidence should be updated regularly in knowledge-evidence to improve the services to achieve the wellbeing and mental fitness of the service-users/survivors. Both qualitative and quantitative researches should not compete even if the right to compete is a modem trend. As aforementioned, objective quantitative data can offer a structure to the evaluation of subjective qualitative data. They must follow the example of the right brain focusing on the subjective aspects thereby often getting into trouble . . .and the left brain dealing with the objective aspects, going to the rescue of the right brain to get its owner out of trouble. Evidence-based mental health practice should be underpinned by the Holistic philosophy in combating mental illness and promoting mental health to service-users/survivors. Is evidence-based mental health practice a far-away dream or a harsh reality?

Word Count: 1,780

References:

1) OU (2004), K272, Challenging Ideas on Mental Health, Module 2, Unit 7,
Whose Evidence? Milton Keynes MK7 6AA

2) Mental Health: Global Policies and Human Rights (2004) by Peter Morrell and Mike Hazelton, Whurr Publishers Ltd., London, (2004)

3) Rod Davies (October 2002) Orient Pacific Century, Asia Market Research
Internet

Character Education

Character education is a vital ingredient in generating respect for others regarding the upbringing of children. Good parental example is the best method of instilling this virtue in the young and not by means of control-conditioning. Behind this virtue, parents should explain to the children the principle of self-respect; for how could the children respect others when they don't know self-respect? Self-knowledge and self-awareness are essential in parents who have children because it is the law of nature that children imbibe the characters of their parents and of those who bring them up during childhood. Children are individuals just as parents are individuals.

According to my interpretation of Jungian psychology, children generate the Indents from their parents, which would be either good or bad. They could show early in life or may be dormant for a while but could be activated by certain stimuli.

In our industrialized society, age-old social ideas and conditions are radically altered. These changes in outlook and social structures prompt the young to question inherited values, thus their minds and consciences become restless and full of disquiet. These changes are often rapid and uncontrolled which disturb their minds. More efficient mass communications bring about keener awareness of contrasts in the world which intensify tension and strain in the minds of the young.

Now, there's environmental pollution brought about by the waste-products created by the rapid advancements of science and technology. Hand-in-hand with economic, scientific and technological progress there is moral and spiritual poverty, as well as a denial of the existence of God by a great number of people. As the outer material (economic, scientific and technological) growth prosper, there is moral and spiritual deprivation in the inner growth of the individuals, as simultaneously, a denial of the existence of God ensues.

Family discords arise due to economic, social and religious problems. There is unequal distribution of material wealth and prosperity amongst families. And, no matter how much control parents exert upon their children, they do rebel. Mutual understanding between parents and children are automatically out-of-reach when there is no self-knowledge and self-awareness amongst parents and children.

Mrs. Antonia Urduja Roberts

Music Within My World Within Worlds

Music is my metaphor. Music generates and sustains rapport. For me, it is a necessity for working at ones best and in the creation of ideal projects such as scientific, psychological and neuroscientific researches conducted by teams of scientists or by lay people.

Mr. Blair once preached about music as an important element that should be included in politics. In the Philippines, music and politics are synonymous. Politics is courtship and music should be intertwined in both. In politics, the candidate courts the voters for their votes and in courtship, Prince Channing serenades his ladylove to capture her heart, through the language of music.

Music is the catalyst. Music, too, softens the soul and invigorates the spirit, it mellows emotional equilibrium and consolidates the mental processes and the short-term memories to long-term memories from within various structures of the brain and in the nervous system, so as to face and undergo the day-to-day challenges of our objective world.

Therefore, Music is my metaphor on the basis of rapport, on working at one's best and on ideal projects. Music in language and in songs! My whole life experiences are tied up in a book that vibrates with the musical cadence of undying verses that I have written Music . . . music . . . music.

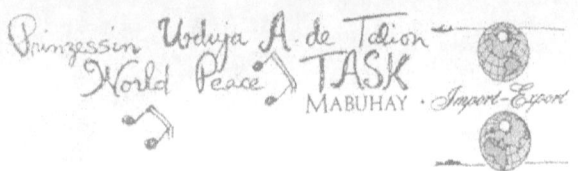

Email From: 'A U Roberts' ------- To: --------------
Sent: 27 May 2004 19:19
Subject: Letter To The Editor English language belong to everyone, says Howard

Daily Telegraph, Wednesday, 26th May 2004,
News Bulletin, page 2

It's the English accent that endears the English language to foreigners. It is Enchantment of its own accord...! It also sings out elegance, pride and dignity without being monotonous. Foreign words should be integrated within the language with slightly altered spellings and accompanying accents from the culture of the country where the words originated from, to provide them with identities.

The German word, "Krankenhaus" is a dichotomy of two parts- "Kranken-sick", "Haus-house" or "House of the sick". The accent for this spoken word denotes sadness...a rather melancholy accent. Accents and emotions go hand-in-hand, tempered with the nervous vibrations of the speakers revealing their individual attributes and character traits. "Ventana" is a Spanish word for "Window." The Filipino language had adopted the same word and meaning but with a different spelling and accent-"Bintana". The accent expresses joy, openness, honesty and trust.

I agree with what Mr. Howard had said that language was the most obvious "binding" element in society. But, multiculturalism in a language would be dead and monotonous without the accompanying individual and cultural accents which signify the different cultural attributes in the mentalities, attitudes, feelings and emotions of the speakers. The mysterious anticipation of the outcomes of multiculturalistic conversations strengthens the more of the language because misunderstandings, in one way or the other, are bound to arise which should, therefore, be followed by explorations of why they had arisen...to promote Goodwill, Peace and Understanding amongst cultures.

The English language is not English without the English accent, but it needs to grow...growth needs liberation in some aspects and growth can be painful too, it's richness does not only spring from its absorption of new words from around the world, but also from the nuances and multitudinal meanings of each word conveyed by the

mentalities, attitudes, feelings, emotions and characters guided by the body language of the foreign speakers. In fact, Accents and Enhanced body language may futuristically render sign-language superfluous!

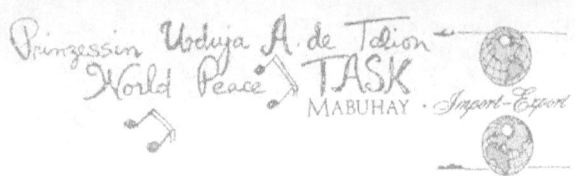

Email From: 'A U Roberts' -------
To: --------------
Sent: 17 October 2002 09:50
Subject: Client Distress

We have a very distressed, 92 year-old, male resident in the Dementia Unit of a nursing home where I work as a night HCA. He was admitted two months ago, due to the recent death of his wife in May 2002. The hospital has told him that she is still alive. Wasn't it unethical, immoral, very childish and very irresponsible to have lied in this manner? Have they ever thought of the consequences of this lie?

Before admission to the nursing home, he was very apprehensive of "fitting-in". shortly afterwards, he started to look for his wife amongst the female residents of the unit. He hopes to have a woman share his bed-he told me several times when I tucked him in bed at night. He made amorous, physical advances to some female residents in the unit and some of them responded. They became his wives, in his imagination!

Occasionally, he got up in the middle of the night feeling angry and jealous, convinced that his wife was sleeping with another man. It was time for him to sort her out, he shouted. He opened all the bedroom doors of the unit looking for his wife. At other times, he suffered from visual hallucinations of his wife and two children standing by his bedside.

During the days, he was very agitated and confused which gave way to violence. He hit several of the female residents, who were his pseudo-wives, with his cane. They acquired bruises on some parts of their bodies and sometimes, they landed on the floor.

He is more settled now. He is not agitated anymore, but is still confused. Violence is not a part of his persona anymore. He is transformed into a kind and understanding old man.

He still looks for his wife sometimes, but we make him realize that she is now in heaven.

Name of Sender: Mrs. Antonia Urduja Talion Roberts

EX CATHEDRA PRAYER For the Fulfillment of the Prophecy of Our Lady of Fatima for World Peace!

OH MY ONE SUPREME BEARER, in Whom Everything is contained and who sustains everything, the Mightiest and the most Supreme of Them and of Us all, Who has both Divine nature and Human nature, Whose Divine nature and Divine Love borne Almighty God the Father, our Creator, God the Son our Redeemer Jesus Christ, God the Holy Spirit, our Sanctificator, and Whose Human nature and Human Love borne the Human Mischief the reconciled Angel, Bearer of Light, Angel Lucifer . . . in union with the Church Triumphant, the Church Militant and the Church Sufferings, a little more of Thine Divine Humanity and of Thine Human Divinity, a little more of Thine most precious blood to run through to my veins to fill my whole being and to keep me going, a little more of Thine most precious breath of Life to fill my whole being and to keep me going. . .continuous Divine guidance, Divine protection, Divine provinence forever and always through all eternity, by the grace of God. That Thou may be able to transubstantiate in us and we may be able to transubstantiate in Thee in accordance with Thine needs and desires, and with our needs, too- through sharing, prayers, good works and frequent reception of the Sacraments through the grace of God. Strength, Courage, Wisdom and the Know-how on how to be able to cope in connection with the acquisition of Gods Divine Wisdom, of Gods Divine Life, Gods Divine Love and Gods Divine Providence... moderation, temperance, gift of knowledge, gift of understanding, Christian sense of justice, gift of tongues as well as other virtues and traits necessary for the execution of Thine Divine Will, such as patience, perseverance, tenacity, equanimity, fortitude, piety, determination, endurance and good health (physical, mental, emotional, intellectual, moral, spiritual) and all other aspects of life. To strengthen me in my/our weaknesses, as a token of Love and Gratitude for the gift of Gods Divine Life, of Gods Divine Love and of Gods Providence and in general, for the Oneness of Divine Nature and Human nature, for the coming of God's Kingdom into this world, for the Peaceful Destiny of Humanity and for the solution to the Mystery of Life Everlasting. Amen.

Please be before me to lead me the Way and to guide me, please be beside me to accompany me and so that I can lean on Thee and tell you my troubles, ideas, values, principles and Thou cans't

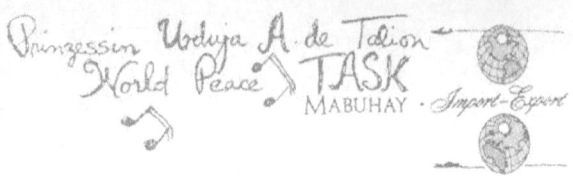

share and counsel me (individual needs...) Please be above me to bless me and please be below me to catch me when I am falling and to pick me up when I have fallen.

Dear Father, Lord and All! Please give me/us the strength to change the things that need changing the courage to accept the things that cannot be changed now but slowly, little by little later on/in the future and the wisdom to know the difference. Hand in hand with that wisdom, please give me/us the strength, the courage, the wisdom and the know-how on how to be able to cope in connection with the acquisition of that wisdom . . . such as patience, perseverance, tenacity, equanimity, fortitude, piety, determination, endurance and good health (physical. mental, emotional, intellectual, moral, spiritual and all other aspects of life) to strengthen me/us in my/our weaknesses, as a token of love and gratitude for the gift of Life, of Love, of Gods Divine Life, of Gods Divine Love and Gods Divine Will and of Gods Divine Providence. . .moderation, temperance, gift of knowledge, gilt of understanding, Christian sense of justice, gift of tongues as well as of other virtues and traits necessary for the execution of Thine Divine and Human Will. . .for the Oneness of Divine nature and Human nature, for the coming of Gods Kingdom into this world, for the peaceful destiny of humanity and for the solution to the mystery of life everlasting. Amen

Prinzessin Urduja A. de Talion, 17 August 2004

www.ingramcontent.com/pod-product-compliance
Lightning Source LLC
Chambersburg PA
CBHW020751160426
43192CB00006B/300